Starter

STUDENT
BOOK

THIRD EDITION

SMART CHOICE

SMART LEARNING
on the page and *on the move*

Ken Wilson / Thomas Healy

OXFORD
UNIVERSITY PRESS

OXFORD
UNIVERSITY PRESS

198 Madison Avenue
New York, NY 10016 USA

Great Clarendon Street, Oxford, OX2 6DP, United Kingdom

Oxford University Press is a department of the University of Oxford.
It furthers the University's objective of excellence in research, scholarship,
and education by publishing worldwide. Oxford is a registered trade
mark of Oxford University Press in the UK and in certain other countries

© Oxford University Press 2016

The moral rights of the author have been asserted

First published in 2016

2020 2019 2018 2017 2016

10 9 8 7 6 5 4 3 2 1

ISBN: 978 0 19 460248 8 (STUDENT BOOK PACK COMPONENT)
ISBN: 978 0 19 460253 2 (STUDENT BOOK PACK)
ISBN: 978 0 19 460257 0 (STUDENT BOOK ACCESS CARD PACK COMPONENT)
ISBN: 978 0 19 460259 4 (STUDENT BOOK ONLINE PRACTICE PACK COMPONENT)

Printed in China

This book is printed on paper from certified and well-managed sources

ACKNOWLEDGMENTS

*The publisher is grateful to those who have given permission to reproduce the following
extracts and adaptations of copyright material: (Use for Music/audio/articles/extracts)*

Illustrations by: 5W Infographics: 14(c), 29 (tl)(tr), 34(t), 58(b), 60(t), 61, 68(t), 69,
94; Barb Bastian: 5, 10; Kenneth Batelman: 57, 86, 90, 112; Harry Briggs: 7,
28, 39, 47, 53, 73, 74, 79; Grace Chen Design and Illustration: 24, 52(t); Jamey
Christoph: 13, 22, 62; Kun-Sung Chung Illustration: 64; Mona Daly/Mendola
Artists: 18(t), 19, 72, 106; Kevin Hopgood: 87, 91; Infomen represented by
Début Art: 9, 35, 81; Scott MacNeill/MacNeill+Macintosh: 12(bl)(tr), 26, 41, 60(c);
Karen Minot: 68(c), 93; Marc Mones/AAA Rep. Unipessoal, Lda: 2, 80(c); Muti/
Folio Art: 21, 29, 50; Greg Paprocki: 20, 44(t), 76, 80(t); Geo Parkin: 18(b), 30, 38,
44(b), 54(t), 66, 67; Redseal represented by Début Art: 36, 56; Gavin Reece/New
Division: 8, 16, 34(b), 40, 42, 48(t), 49, 78, 82; Lucy Truman/New Division: 14(b),
32; William Waitzman: 48(c), 52(b), 54(t), 58(t), 59.

*We would also like to thank the following for permission to reproduce the following
photographs:* Cover: Martin Barraud/Getty Images; Mint Images/Tim Pannell/
Getty Images; 4x6/iStockphoto. iii page: martellostudio/iStockphoto (computer);
lvcandy/iStockphoto (phone); RekaReka/iStockphoto (tablet). Inside Back Cover:
lvcandy/iStockphoto (phone). Back Cover: RekaReka/iStockphoto (tablet).
Steven Ogilvy Photography, 3 (teacher); 3 (teacher); 3 (teacher); 3 (teacher);
Photodisc, 3 (strawberry); Photodisc, 4 (teacher); Mark Davis/Getty Images For
BET, 4 (singer); Fancy/Alamy Stock Photo, 4 (writer); Ariel Skelley/Blend Images,
4 (artist); Christian Bertrand/Shutterstock, 4 (actor); Ariel Skelley/Getty Images,
4 (businesswoman); Tetra Images/Alamy Stock Photo, 4 (server); SunKids/
Shutterstock, 4 (student); manfeiyang/Shutterstock, 4 (web designer); Tetra
Images/Getty Images, 4 (chef); Joana Lopes/Shutterstock, 4 (woman); Location
photography by Mannicmedia, 5 (conversation); Paul Harris, PacificCoastNews/
Newscom, 6 (designer); © Armando Gallo/Corbis, 6 (actor); © Antoine Gyori/
AGP/Corbis, 6 (businessman); David Levenson/Getty Images, 6 (writer); Choi
Soo-Young/Multi-Bits via Getty Images, 6 (singer); jeremy sutton-hibbert/Alamy
Stock Photo, 6 (chef); Luis Molinero/Shutterstock, 9 (South Korea); 9 (Brazil); 9
(Canada); 9 (United Kingdom); CS5/C.Smith/ WENN/Newscom, 9 (Taylor Swift);
Comstock/Getty Images, 9 (server); REUTERS/Eric Gaillard, 9 (One Direction);
VSummers / Splash News/Newscom, 9 (Daniel Radcliffe); Stasique/Shutterstock,
10 (male); Bullstar/Shutterstock, 10 (lab); TravnikovStudio/Shutterstock, 10
(pool); El Nariz/Shutterstock, 10 (pizza); Laura Niemuth/Shutterstock, 10
(lake); Location photography by Mannicmedia, 11 (conversation); AVAVA/
Shutterstock, 11 (man); leungchopan/Shutterstock, 12 (Alice Oark); Dima
Sidelnikov/Shutterstock, 12 (Eric Fox); George Doyle/Stockbyte/Getty Images,
12 (Dave Gomez); racorn/Shutterstock, 12 (Amy West); A Aleksii/Shutterstock,
14 (swimming); 14 (photography); 14 (tennis); Blan-k/Shutterstock, 14 (cycling);
oasis15/Shutterstock, 15 (guitar); vixenkristy/Shutterstock, 15 (icecream cone);
Hans Kim/Shutterstock, 16 (woman); Location photography by Mannicmedia,
17 (conversation); Andriy Mertsalov/Shutterstock, 20 (black tablet); 20 (green
tablet); 20 (red tablet); 20 (blue tablet); 20 (white tablet); 20 (gray tablet);
Jeff Kravitz/FilmMagic/Getty Images, 23 (Emilia Clarke); Everett Collection/
Shutterstock, 23 (Beyonce); © Jim Wright/Corbis Outline, 23 (Rachael Ray);
Gilbert Garrigue/Getty Images, 23 (Affeck brothers); Location photography
by Mannicmedia, 25 (conversation); Aila Images/Shutterstock, 25 (man);
Chromakey/Shutterstock, 27 (guitar); julie deshaies/Shutterstock, 27 (drums);
kak2s/Shutterstock, 27 (piano); Vereshchagin Dmitry/Shutterstock, 27
(trumpet); ITAR-TASS Photo Agency/Alamy Stock Photo, 29 (Shakira); REUTERS/
Jo Yong-Hak, 29 (K Pop); VLIET/iStock, 29 (concert dancing); wavebreakmedia/
Shutterstock, 30 (woman), Location photography by Mannicmedia, 31
(conversation); Radius Images/Punchstock, 33 (yoga); Location photography
by Mannicmedia, 37 (conversation); leungchopan/Shutterstock, 37 (man);
Punchstock/Ingram Publishing, 40 (playing guitar); PeopleImages/iStock, 40
(tennis); Stockbyte/Getty Images, 40 (singing); Trinette Reed/Getty Images,
40 (cooking); Donato Sardella/Getty Images, 43 (Jessica and Krystal Jung);
Burberry via Getty Images, 43 (Jessica Jung); © Imaginechina/Corbis, 43
(Krystal Jung); melis/Shutterstock, 43 (stage lights); Joana Lopes/Shutterstock,
44 (woman); Location photography by Mannicmedia, 45 (conversation);
ffongbeer69/Shutterstock, 46 (drinking); Ultimage Group, LLC/Alamy Stock
Photo, 46 (basketball); Image 100 Photo/Punchstock, 46 (shopping); © Kai
Chiang/Golden Pixels LLC/Corbis, 46 (western boots); Stockbyte/PunchStock,
46 (hamburger); Photo Alto/Punchstock, 46 (talking on phone); Location
photography by Mannicmedia, 51 (conversation); AVAVA/Shutterstock,
51 (man); Photofusion /Getty Images, 55 (messy room); Tara Moore/Getty
Images, 55 (decorated room); Hans Kim/Shutterstock, 56 (woman); Location
photography by Mannicmedia, 57 (conversation); X.D. Luo/Shutterstock,
63 (woman); August/Shutterstock, 63 (room); Banana Stock/PunchStock, 63
(hotel); Location photography by Mannicmedia, 65 (conversation); Aila Images/
Shutterstock, 65 (man); Brain Weed/Shutterstock, 66 (coffee); Punchstock, 66
(cookie); Foodcollection.com/Punchstock, 66 (potatoes); John A Rizzo/Photodisc/
PunchStock, 66 (pasta); Joe Gough/Shutterstock, 66 (bread); Photodisc, 66
(apple); ktphotog/iStockphoto, 66 (milk); Hemera Collection, 66 (bananas);
Lew Robertson/StockFood Creative/Getty Images, 66 (chicken); DAJ,70 (gym);
newphotoservice/Shutterstock, 70 (library); Sir Armstrong/Shutterstock,
70 (home); Jack Hollingsworth/Getty Images, 70 (school); Lane Oate/Getty
Images, 70 (work); Fuse/Getty Images, 70 (laundromat); iofoto/Shutterstock,
70 (supermarket); V. J. Matthew/Shutterstock, 70 (mall); wavebreakmedia/
Shutterstock, 70 (woman); Location photography by Mannicmedia, 71
(conversation); Thomas Abraham/iStock, 74 (office); James Forte/Getty Images,
74 (doctor's office); wavebreakmedia/Shutterstock, 74 (library); Rabyesang/
Shutterstock, 74 (mall); Radu Bercan/Shutterstock, 75 (bookstore); Maureen
Sullivan/Getty Images, 75 (laundromat); baona/iStock, 75 (store); Location
photography by Mannicmedia, 77 (conversation); leungchopan/Shutterstock,
77 (man); Andresr/Shutterstock, 83 (Linda Porter); arek_malang/Shutterstock,
83 (Brian Chan); Danny E Hooks/Shutterstock, 83 (Carla Lewis); Purestock/
PunchStock, 84 (Mike Johnson); Comstock/Alamy Stock Photo, 84 (Julia Rivera);
BananaStock/Robert Stock, 84 (Amy Hooper); © Blue Jean Images/Corbis, 84
(Richard Wong); Ann Perchevskaja/Shutterstock, 85 (background); Brand X/
PunchStock, 85 (Alan); Fancy/Veer, 85 (Meg); Blend Images/PunchStock, 85
(Kazu and Hiro); Image Source/PunchStock, 85 (Jen); Purestock/PunchStock, 88
(Mike Johnson); Comstock/Alamy Stock Photo, 88 (Julia Rivera); BananaStock/
Robert Stock, 88 (Amy Hooper); © Blue Jean Images/Corbis, 88 (Richard Wong);
Ann Perchevskaja/Shutterstock, 89 (background); Brand X/PunchStock, 89
(Alan); Fancy/Veer, 89 (Meg); Blend Images/PunchStock, 89 (Kazu and Hiro);
Image Source/PunchStock, 89 (Jen); Jeffrey Mayer/Getty Images, 92 (on stage);
Melamory/Shutterstock, 92 (background); © Christopher Ameruoso/Splash
News/Corbis, 92 (with dog); © Larsen & Talbert/Corbis Outline, 92 (on rug);
Randal Ford/Somos Images/Corbis, 93 (Ellen); g-stockstudio/Shutterstock, 93
(Keith and Matt); Rich Legg/iStock, 93 (David); Brand X Pictures/PunchStock, 93
(Aiko); Kelly Redinger/Vibe Images/Alamy Stock Photo, 93 (Mark and Jennifer);
© 2/Mel Yates/Ocean/Corbis, 94 (karaoke); 94 (karaoke inset); marchello74/
Shutterstock, 95 (beach); luoman/iStock, 95 (mountain); Globe Stock/Alamy
Stock Photo, 95 (museum). RekaReka/iStockphoto (tablet). Inside Back Cover:
lvcandy/iStockphoto (phone). Back Cover: RekaReka/iStockphoto (tablet).

NEW
FOR SMART CHOICE!

More ways to keep learning outside the classroom.

ONLINE PRACTICE

Use your computer to practice all four skills and communicate with your class with Online Practice.

- Connect with your teacher and classmates, get feedback, and track your progress
- 30 hours of additional practice, indicated on the Student Book pages

ON THE MOVE

Use your smartphone or tablet to practice anywhere with NEW On The Move activities.

- Extend learning with five activities for each unit
- Practice your vocabulary, grammar, and listening skills
- Receive instant feedback and improve your score

◀ On The Move activities are optimized for use on smartphones.

 Plus download or stream all the Student Book and Workbook audio and video to practice listening wherever you are!

GET STARTED

See the inside back cover of your Student Book to get started.

SCOPE AND SEQUENCE

▶ LISTENING	READING & WRITING	LEARNING TIPS	LEARNING OUTCOMES
• **Listening 1:** Introductions • **Listening Plus:** People asking for more information about each other	• **Reading:** Occupations • **Writing:** A letter about your partner's personal information (p. 92)	• **Vocabulary:** Keeping a vocabulary notebook	• Make an introduction • Make statements and questions with *be* • Understand basic information about people • Understand what people do
• **Listening 1:** People asking for and giving personal information • **Listening Plus:** More questions about a person's personal information	• **Reading:** Personal details • **Writing:** A letter about your partner's personal information (p. 92)	• **Conversation:** Playing an active role	• Answer questions about myself and others • Use possessives and *wh-* questions • Understand short conversations about people • Understand personal details in forms
• **Listening 1:** Two people asking and talking about photos and possessions • **Listening Plus:** More questions about the people and possessions in the photos	• **Reading:** Personal possessions • **Writing:** A letter about your partner's personal information (p. 92)	• **Vocabulary:** Learning the spelling of new words	• Talk about things I have • Use *this, that, these,* and *those* • Understand what other people have • Understand phrases about possessions
• **Listening 1:** People talking about the music they like • **Listening Plus:** People talking about their favorite types of music	• **Reading:** Likes and dislikes • **Writing:** A letter about your friends (p. 93)	• **Conversation:** Being polite	• Talk about likes and dislikes • Use the simple present with *like* • Understand what types of music people like • Understand phrases about likes and dislikes
• **Listening 1:** People talking about weekend activities • **Listening Plus:** People talking about more weekend activities	• **Reading:** What do you do for fun? • **Writing:** A letter about your friends (p. 93)	• **Vocabulary:** Making sentences with new words	• Suggest things to do with someone • Use the simple present • Understand what people do in their free time • Understand what people do for fun
• **Listening 1:** People talking about what they can and can't do • **Listening Plus:** People talking about what they can do well	• **Reading:** People's abilities • **Writing:** A letter about your friends (p. 93)	• **Conversation:** Giving more details	• Talk about abilities • Use *can* and *can't* to talk about abilities • Understand people saying what they can do • Understand phrases about what people can do

SCOPE AND SEQUENCE

► LISTENING	READING & WRITING	LEARNING TIPS	LEARNING OUTCOMES
• **Listening 1:** People describing themselves and other people • **Listening Plus:** People talking about what they're doing right now	• **Reading:** What people are doing • **Writing:** A text message about what you are doing (p. 94)	• **Vocabulary:** Making a picture dictionary	• Talk about what is happening now • Use the present continuous • Understand what people are wearing • Understand what people are doing
• **Listening 1:** People asking and talking about where things are located • **Listening Plus:** People asking about where more things are located	• **Reading:** Describing rooms • **Writing:** A text message about what you are doing (p. 94)	• **Conversation:** Confirming information	• Describe what is in my home • Use *there is* and *there are* • Understand where things are in a home • Understand short descriptions of rooms
• **Listening 1:** People preparing recipes • **Listening Plus:** People talking about what they need to prepare a recipe	• **Reading:** Directions • **Writing:** A text message about what you are doing (p. 94)	• **Vocabulary:** Making a word-of-the-day calendar	• Give and follow short, simple directions • Describe locations and give directions • Listen and follow directions on a map • Understand directions on a map
• **Listening 1:** People asking for directions • **Listening Plus:** A person asking for detailed directions to a specific place	• **Reading:** Food and drink • **Writing:** A letter about a trip (p. 95)	• **Conversation:** Being polite	• Talk about food and drink • Use count/noncount nouns and *some/any* • Understand what is needed to make recipes • Understand phrases about food and drinks
• **Listening 1:** People talking about where they were • **Listening Plus:** People asking for and giving more information about where they were	• **Reading:** Past activities and places • **Writing:** A letter about a trip (p. 95)	• **Vocabulary:** Making sentences with new words	• Talk about where you were • Use the past tense of *be* • Understand where people were • Understand where people were last week
• **Listening 1:** People talking about their weekend • **Listening Plus:** People asking for and giving more information about their weekend	• **Reading:** Past activities • **Writing:** A letter about a trip (p. 95)	• **Conversation:** Turn-taking	• Talk about past activities • Use the simple past tense • Understand past weekend activities • Understand phrases about past activities

SMART TALK	WRITING	AUDIO SCRIPTS	GRAMMAR REFERENCE & PRACTICE	VOCABULARY
Pages 84–91	Pages 92–95	Pages 96–103	Pages 104–115	Pages 116–117

vii

VOCABULARY

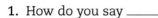 **1** Listen and repeat.

1. How do you say _____ in English?

2. How do you spell _____?

3. How do you say this word?

4. What does _____ mean?

5. Excuse me, can you repeat that, please?
   I'm sorry, I don't understand.
   I'm sorry, can you speak more slowly?

CONVERSATION

1 Complete the conversations with the phrases in the box.
Then listen and check your answers.

Can you repeat that?	How do you pronounce this word?
How do you spell that?	What's this called in English?
What does *delighted* mean?	

1. **A** <u>How do you pronounce this word?</u>
   B Which one? This one?
   A Uh-huh. That one.
   B Favorite.

2. **A** _____
   B It means "very happy."

3. **A** _____
   B That? That's called a keychain.
   A Sorry. _____
   B Sure. Keychain.

4. **A** How do you say 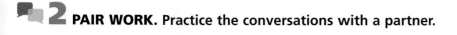 in English?
   B Strawberry.
   A _____
   B Strawberry? S-T-R-A-W-B-E-R-R-Y.

2 **PAIR WORK.** Practice the conversations with a partner.

1 I'm a student.

SPEAKING	GRAMMAR	LISTENING	READING
Introducing yourself	The verb *be*	Meeting people	Occupations

WARM UP
Introduce yourself to your partner.

VOCABULARY

1 Look at the people. What are their jobs? Write the correct letter.

a. a singer	f. a server
b. an actor	g. a businesswoman
c. an artist	h. a student
d. a writer	i. a chef
e. a teacher	j. a web designer

1.

2.

3.

4.

5.

6.

7.

8.

9.

10.

ONLINE PRACTICE

2 Listen and check your answers.

3 PAIR WORK. Practice spelling the words above.

Spell _chef_.

C-H-E-F. Spell _student_.

VOCABULARY TIP
Write down new words in a notebook.

artist
businesswoman
server

CONVERSATION

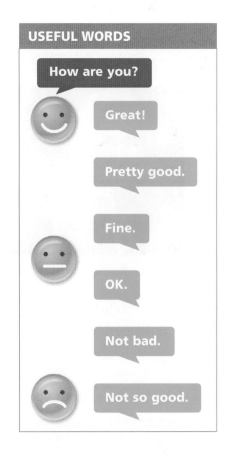

USEFUL WORDS

How are you?

Great!

Pretty good.

Fine.

OK.

Not bad.

Not so good.

1 Listen to the conversations and repeat. Practice the conversations with a partner.

1. Anthony   Hi. I'm <u>Anthony</u>. Nice to meet you.
    Mrs. Davis My name's <u>Mrs. Davis</u>. Nice to meet you, too.
    Anthony   Are you from <u>New York</u>, <u>Mrs. Davis</u>?
    Mrs. Davis Yes, I am. How about you?
    Anthony   I'm from <u>Vancouver</u>.

2. Mrs. Davis Hello, <u>Anthony</u>.
    Anthony   Oh, hi, <u>Mrs. Davis</u>. How are you?
    Mrs. Davis <u>Not bad</u>, thanks. How about you?
    Anthony   <u>Good</u>, thanks.
    Mrs. Davis Well, class is about to start, so please take your seat.
    Anthony   Oh, uh… sure thing!

2 **PAIR WORK.** Practice the conversations again.
Use information about you for the underlined words.

Hi, I'm Marco. Nice to meet you.

My name's Lisa. Nice to meet you, too.

LANGUAGE PRACTICE

Statements with *be*			Grammar Reference page 104
I'm Sara.	I am → I'm	**I'm not** a student	I am not → I'm not
You're a student.	You are → You're	**He isn't** a teacher.	isn't → is not
He's a server.	He is → He's		My name is → My name's
She's an actor.	She is → She's		

ONLINE PRACTICE

1 Look at the pictures. Complete the sentences. Then listen and check your answers.

Jonathan Ive, designer

Scarlett Johansson, actor

Bill Gates, businessman

1. Jonathan Ive
   ___isn't___ a writer.
   ___He's___ a designer.

2. Scarlett Johansson
   _____ a chef.
   _____ an actor.

3. Bill Gates _____
   a businessman.
   He _____ a student.

J. K. Rowling, writer

Ailee, singer

Gordon Ramsay, chef

4. J. K. Rowling _____
   a teacher.
   _____ a writer.

5. Ailee _____ a singer.
   She _____ a web
   designer.

6. Gordon Ramsay
   _____ a server.
   _____ a chef.

2 Tell your class about yourself.

Hi. I'm Rosa. I'm from Mexico City. I'm a student.

Hello. I'm David. I'm a server. I'm from Paris.

Hi. I'm _____.

Yes/no questions with be

Grammar Reference page 104

ONLINE PRACTICE

Are you a teacher?	Yes, **I am.**/No, **I'm not.**
Is he a chef?	Yes, **he is.**/No, **he isn't.**
Are they from Tokyo?	Yes, **they are.**/No, **they aren't.**

3 Complete the conversations. Use information about you for the last one.

1. A ___Are___ you from Rio?
   B Yes, I ___am___.

2. A _____ you a teacher?
   B No, _____ not.
   _____ a student.

3. A Is _____ a chef?
   B No, he _____. He's a server.

4. A _____ a designer?
   B Yes, she _____.

5. A _____ they from Toronto?
   B No, they _____. _____ from London.

6. A _____?
   B _____.

4 **PAIR WORK.** Practice the conversation with a partner. Use information about you.

PRONUNCIATION—*Reduction of* a/an

1 Listen. Notice the reduced sounds of *a* and *an*.

Unreduced	Reduced		Unreduced	Reduced
1. I'm a student.	*Imuh* student.		3. He's a server.	*Hezuh* server.
2. You're a teacher.	*Youruh* teacher.		4. She's an actor.	*Shezuhn* actor.

2 Listen again and repeat. Be sure to reduce *a* and *an*.

7

LISTENING

1 **BEFORE YOU LISTEN** **Which of these jobs do you like? Check the pictures.**

1. a programmer   2. a tour guide   3. a model   4. an engineer

2 **Listen to the people talking. Which picture are they in? Number the pictures below.**

A.   B.   C.   D.

3 **Listen again. Complete the sentences. Use the words in the box.**

Tom Cruise   an engineer   Canada   a student

1. Sara isn't from the US. She's from __Canada__.
2. John is _____.
3. The man isn't _____. He's Brad Pitt.
4. Paula isn't a businesswoman. She's _____.

4 **Listening PLUS. Listen to more of Paula and Ted's conversation. Choose (✓) True or False.**

	True	False
1. Paula isn't from the US.	☐	☐
2. Ted is from New York.	☐	☐

SPEAKING — *Are you from South Korea?*

1 Read the instructions below to play the game.

1. Play the game in pairs or groups.
2. Choose an object as a game piece.
3. Use a coin to move. Heads = 1 space.
   Tails = 2 spaces.
4. Take turns asking and answering questions.

 South Korea   **Brazil**

 Canada   **United Kingdom**

> **Is Taylor Swift a model?**

> No, she isn't. She's a singer.

2 **PAIR WORK.** Now play the game. Who is the winner?

START

 **1** Is Taylor Swift a model?

 **2** Are you from South Korea?

 **3** Please spell.

4 Make a question.

7 Make a question.

 6 Is your teacher from Canada?

 **5** Is the band One Direction from Brazil?

 **8** Are you a teacher?

 **9** Is Daniel Radcliffe a singer?

10 Make a question.

FINISH

GO ONLINE Find information about your favorite celebrity. Tell your classmates.

NOW I CAN

SPEAKING	GRAMMAR	LISTENING	READING
✓ make an introduction.	☐ make statements and questions with *be*.	☐ understand basic information about people.	☐ understand what people do.

2 What's your phone number?

SPEAKING Personal information / **GRAMMAR** Possessives/Questions / **LISTENING** Personal information / **READING** Personal details

WARM UP
When is your birthday?

VOCABULARY

1 Look at the pictures. What do they mean? Write the correct letter.

a. email address	c. birthday	e. address	g. favorite food	i. nickname
b. hobby	d. major	f. phone number	h. favorite singer	j. hometown

Daniel Williams **About Me**

1. ___ Dan
2. ___ New York
3. ___ June 15th
4. ___ 123 Madison Street
5. ___ 345-8932
6. ___ dan321@inter.net
7. ___ pizza
8. ___ Pharrell Williams
9. ___ chemistry
10. ___ painting

ONLINE PRACTICE

2 Listen and check your answers.

3 PAIR WORK. **Take turns saying and writing down the words above. Check that your partner wrote the words correctly.**

USEFUL LANGUAGE
@ = "at"
.com = "dot com"

CONVERSATION

1 Complete the conversation. Then listen and check your answers. Practice the conversation with a partner.

a. chemistry	b. pizza	c. Vancouver

Anthony OK, Kelly. I'm ready for the interview.

Kelly Great! So, Anthony, what's your favorite food?

Anthony My favorite food is ⟨1 ⟩.

Kelly Me, too! And what's your major?

Anthony My major is ⟨2 ⟩.

Kelly Really? I'm a biology major. What's your hometown?

Anthony I'm from ⟨3 ⟩.

Kelly That's my favorite place!

Anthony So... what's your phone number?

2 **PAIR WORK.** Practice the conversation again. Use the ideas below. Add your own ideas.

1	2	3
sushi	history	Tokyo
Mexican food	math	Acapulco
_____	_____	_____

CONVERSATION TIP

PLAY AN ACTIVE ROLE
Use agreement statements to keep active in a conversation.

My favorite food is pizza.

Me, too!

11

LANGUAGE PRACTICE

Possessives　　　　　　　　　　　　　　　　　　　**Grammar Reference page 105**

My favorite food is pizza.
Your email address is tom_garcia@webmail.net.
His/Her major is chemistry.
Our phone number is 555–7612.
Their address is 710 Dock Street.
Dan's hobby is hiking.

Saying email addresses
@ → "at"
.com → "dot com"
.edu → "dot e-d-u"
– → "dash"
_ → "underscore"

ONLINE PRACTICE

1 Look at the pictures. Complete the sentences. Then listen and check your answers.

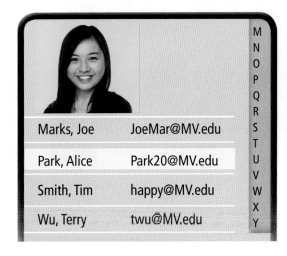

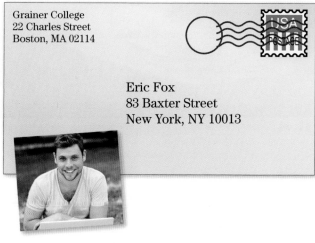

1. __Her__ name __is__ Alice Park.　　2. _____ address _____ 83 Baxter Street.

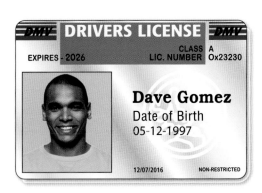

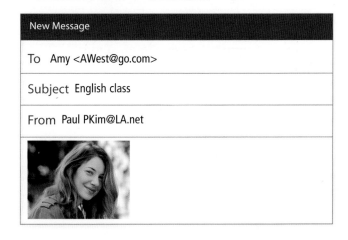

3. _____ birthday _____ May 12th.　　4. _____ email address _____ AWest@go.com.

2 PAIR WORK. Imagine a new name, address, and email address. Take turns telling your information and completing this name card for your partner.

> I'm Elvis Neymar.
> My address is 350 5th Avenue,
> New York, NY 10118.

Name _____
Address _____　Phone _____

12

Wh– questions with *be*

Grammar Reference page 105

What's your name?	My name's Alice.
What's their email address?	It's smile21 @inter.net.
Where's he from?	He's from Kyoto.
When's her birthday?	It's August 4th.
Who's your favorite singer?	It's Madonna.

ONLINE PRACTICE

3 Match the questions and answers.

1. What's his name? _d_
2. What's her address? ___
3. What's Anna's email address? ___
4. Who's your favorite singer? ___
5. When's his birthday? ___
6. Where are they from? ___

a. They're from Mexico.
b. It's 412 Park Avenue.
c. It's Elvis Presley.
d. His name's Paul.
e. It's anna7@webmail.net.
f. It's December 17th.

4 PAIR WORK. Complete the questions. Then practice the conversation. Use information about you.

1. A ___What's your___ favorite food?
   B My favorite food is ___pizza___.
2. A _____ our teacher from?
   B _____ from _____.
3. A _____ birthday?
   B It's _____.
4. A _____ favorite singer?
   B My favorite singer is _____.

PRONUNCIATION—*Saying phone numbers and email addresses*

1 Listen. Notice the pauses between the groups of numbers. Then listen again and repeat.

1. (987) 525-6712
2. (265) 725-6388
3. (03) 3459-0390
4. (0141) 36-2395

2 Listen. Notice how these email addresses are pronounced. Then listen again and repeat.

1. dan.rogers@internet.co.uk
2. ariel_wu@torontodesign.co.ca

LISTENING

1 **BEFORE YOU LISTEN** Which of these things do you do? Check the pictures.

1. swimming   2. photography   3. cycling   4. tennis

2 Listen to the people talking. Complete the pictures with the correct information.

1.

8:50 AM
Incoming call
327- ___ ___ ___ ___
0:25

2.

3:33 PM
Contacts
Jones, Mike
Email: _____
Jordan, Dave
Josephs, Ann
H I J K L M N O P

3.

12:34 PM
Contacts
Takeda, Kyoko
Address: _____ Park Street
Thompson, John
R S T U V W X

4.

LICENSE DMV
CLASS C
LIC. NUMBER 3X39746
DANA OWENS
DATE OF BIRTH ___ ___ 1985

3 Listen again. Choose (✓) *True* or *False*.

	True	False
1. Swimming is Fiona's favorite hobby.	☐	☐
2. Michael's nickname is Mike.	☐	☐
3. Kyoko's telephone number is 524-9056.	☐	☐
4. Today is Dana's birthday.	☐	☐

4 **Listening PLUS.** Listen to more of Fiona's conversation. Complete the chart.

Fiona's personal information	
1.	Home phone number	
2.	Address	
3.	Birthday	
4.	Driver's license number	

SPEAKING — *Class directory*

1 Complete the chart below with information about you.

Nickname	Major	Hobbies	Favorite Food	Favorite Singer or Band

2 **GROUP WORK.** Complete the class directory with information about your classmates.

Example

> Is your name Charles?

> Yes, it is.

> What's your nickname?

> It's Chuck.

	Nickname	Major	Hobbies	Favorite Food	Favorite Singer or Band
1.					
2.					
3.					
4.					
5.					
6.					

3 **CLASS ACTIVITY.** What did you learn about your classmates? Share your information with the class.

> Makiko's favorite band is One Direction.

GO ONLINE Find three personal details about your favorite singer. Tell your classmates.

NOW I CAN

SPEAKING	GRAMMAR	LISTENING	READING
☐ answer questions about myself and others.	☐ use possessives and *wh-* questions.	☐ understand short conversations about people.	☐ understand personal details in forms.

15

3 That's my wallet!

SPEAKING / **GRAMMAR** / **LISTENING** / **READING**
Things you have / *This/that, these/those* / Things people have / Personal possessions

WARM UP
What things do you have in your bag?

VOCABULARY

1 Look at the picture. Write the correct letter.

a. a driver's license	c. glasses	e. money	g. a wallet	i. a school ID card
b. keys	d. a cell phone	f. an ATM card	h. headphones	j. textbooks

2 Listen and check your answers.

3 **PAIR WORK.** Look at the picture for one minute. Then close your book. How many words can you remember?

> Wallet, cell phone, glasses...

VOCABULARY TIP
Practice spelling new words to learn them.

> *glasses*
> *glasses*
> *glasses*

16

CONVERSATION

ONLINE
PRACTICE

◄))) **1** **Complete the conversation. Then listen and check your answers. Practice the conversation with a partner.**

| a. ID card | b. wallet | c. photos |

Man	Can I help you?
Kelly	Yes, please. Is that my 1 [ ] ?
Man	Just a moment. What's your name?
Kelly	Kelly. Kelly Yamada.
Man	Yes, this is your card. Here you are.
Kelly	Thank you. Oh, I think those are my 2 [ ] .
Man	These? Oh, yes, they are. Anything else?
Kelly	Yes... that's my 3 [ ] .
Man	Here you are. And is that your bag?
Kelly	No, this is my bag. Thanks!

💬**2** **PAIR WORK. Practice the conversation again. Use the ideas below. Add your own ideas.**

1	2	3
driver's license	keys	money
credit card	glasses	cell phone
_____	_____	_____

LANGUAGE PRACTICE

 This and *that*   Grammar Reference page 106

This is my camera.

Is this your wallet?

Is that your car?

Who's this?

Who's that?

That's her camera.

Yes, **it is**./No, **it isn't**.

Yes, **it is**./No, **it isn't**.

It's my sister.

It's my mother.   Who is → Who's

 ONLINE PRACTICE

1 Look at the pictures. Complete the conversations. Then listen and check your answers.

1. **A** Is ___this___ your camera?
   B Yes, it is. Thank you!

2. **A** Who's _____?
   B It's my teacher.

3. **A** Is this your car?
   B No, it isn't. _____ my car.

4. **A** Is that your dog?
   B No, _____ _____. Run!

2 **PAIR WORK.** Draw three items in the box. Then ask and answer questions with your partner.

Is that a *dog* **?**

No, it isn't.

Is that a _____ **?**

These and *those*

These are my photos.
Are these your photos?
Are those your sisters?
Who are these girls?
Who are those people?

Grammar Reference page 106

Those are my photos.
Yes, **they are.**/No, **they aren't.**
Yes, **they are.**/No, **they aren't.**
They're my sisters.
They're my neighbors.

3 Match the questions and answers.

1. Are these your photos? _b_
2. Are these your classmates? ___
3. Who are those people? ___
4. How old are those men? ___

a. They're my brothers.
b. Yes, they are.
c. They are 22 and 19.
d. No, they aren't. They're my friends.

4 **PAIR WORK. Complete the conversations. Then practice them with a partner.**

1. A Are __those__ your parents?
   B Yes, _____ _____.

2. A Are those people your neighbors?
   B _____. They're my family.

3. A Are _____ your keys?
   B No, _____ _____. My keys
   are in my bag.

4. A Are these your books?
   B _____, _____ are.

PRONUNCIATION—*Number pairs*

1 Listen. Practice saying these numbers.

11	12	13	14	15	16	17	18	19	20
eleven	twelve	thirteen	fourteen	fifteen	sixteen	seventeen	eighteen	nineteen	twenty

21	22	30	40	50	60	70	80	90	100
twenty-one	twenty-two	thirty	forty	fifty	sixty	seventy	eighty	ninety	one hundred

2 Listen. Choose the number you hear.

1. 13   30
2. 17   70
3. 15   50
4. 19   90

19

LISTENING

1 **BEFORE YOU LISTEN** Which of these colors do you like? Check the colors.

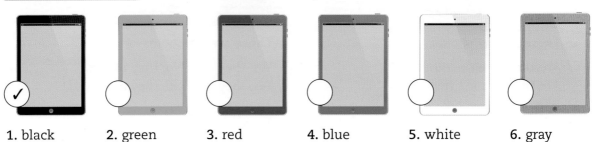

1. black   2. green   3. red   4. blue   5. white   6. gray

2 Listen to May describe her photos. Write the correct number.

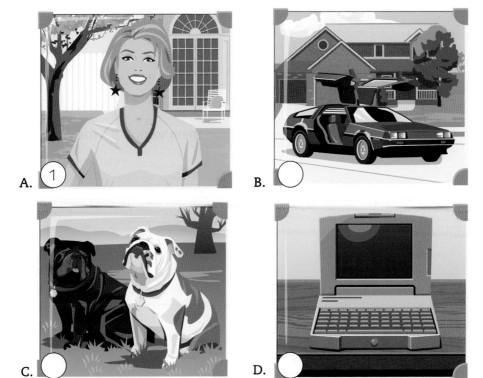

A. ①   B. ○

C. ○   D. ○

3 Listen again. Choose (✓) *True* or *False*.

	True	False
1. Linda is from Brazil.	☐	☐
2. Tina's dog is white.	☐	☐
3. This is May's first computer.	☐	☐
4. This is May's car.	☐	☐

4 **Listening PLUS**. Listen to May say more about her photos. Choose the numbers you hear.

1. a. 22   b. 32   c. 33   3. a. 15   b. 50   c. 16
2. a. 25   b. 39   c. 29   4. a. 35   b. 39   c. 25

SPEAKING — *That's mine!*

1 **ROLE PLAY.** Take turns asking for things in the lost and found office. Student A, ask about items 1, 3, and 5. Student B, ask about items 2, 4, and 6.

> Can you help me? I think that's my bag.

> The red bag?

> No, the blue bag. And I think these are my glasses.

> The black glasses?

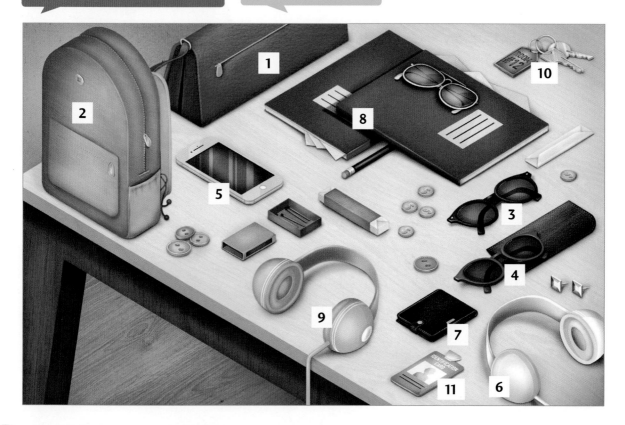

2 **GROUP WORK.** Put three things on a desk in the middle. Take turns guessing whose things they are.

> Is that your wallet, Steve?

> Yes, it is. Karen, are those your glasses?

> No, they aren't.

GO ONLINE Find out what things people usually lose. Where do they lose them? Tell your classmates.

NOW I CAN

SPEAKING	GRAMMAR	LISTENING	READING
☐ talk about things I have.	☐ use *this, that, these,* and *those.*	☐ understand what other people have.	☐ understand phrases about possessions.

21

1 Read the conversation. Choose the correct answer.

Ricardo   Excuse me! *Is this / Are these*
                                1
                    your glasses?

So-young   Yes, they *are / is*. Thanks!
                            2

Ricardo   And is this your comb?

So-young   Yes, it is. Thank you! *Are you / You are*
                                          3
                    in my English class?

Ricardo   Yes, I am. My name's Ricardo. Nice to
                    meet you.

So-young   I'm So-young. Nice to meet you, too.
                    Where are you from, Ricardo?

Ricardo   I'm from Brazil. How *about / are* you?
                                          4

So-young   I'm from South Korea.

Ricardo   Are you from Seoul?

So-young   No, *I'm not / I isn't*. My hometown
                           5
                    is Busan.

Ricardo   My favorite food is Korean food!

So-young   Really? That's my favorite food, too!

Ricardo   Hey, *who's / what's* your cell
                                6
                    phone number?

So-young   It's 230-555-0283.

2 Listen and check your answers. Then practice the conversation with a partner.

3 **PAIR WORK.** Put a box around the countries, cities, and nationalities and the possessions. Practice the conversation again. Use your own ideas for the countries, cities, and nationalities and possessions.

SMART TALK

What's his phone number?   Student A: Turn to page 84.
                                     Student B: Turn to page 88.

4 Look at the pictures. Do you know these people?

FAMOUS NAMES

Emilia Clarke

This is Emilia Clarke. She is an actor. Her hometown is London, England. Her nickname is "Milly." She has a dog. Its name is Roxy.

Beyoncé

This is Beyoncé. She's a singer. Beyoncé's hometown is Houston, Texas, in the US. Her first name is interesting. Beyoncé's birthday is September 4th.

Rachael Ray

This is Rachael Ray. She's from New York. She's a chef, writer, and businesswoman. She loves dogs. Her company makes dog food.

Ben and Casey Affleck

Are these two friends? No, they aren't. They're brothers. Ben and Casey Affleck are actors. Ben is a nickname. His real name is Benjamin. Ben's birthday is August 15th. Casey's birthday is August 12th.

5 Read the article. Choose (✓) *True* or *False*.

	True	False
1. "Milly" is a nickname.	☐	☐
2. Beyoncé is a chef.	☐	☐
3. Beyoncé's hometown is Houston.	☐	☐
4. Rachael Ray is a businessperson.	☐	☐
5. Ben and Casey Affleck are friends.	☐	☐
6. Ben Affleck is a singer.	☐	☐

6 **GROUP WORK.** Who is your favorite singer or actor? Tell your group.

WRITING

Turn to page 92.

23

4 Do you like hip-hop?

SPEAKING Likes and dislikes / **GRAMMAR** Simple present: *like* / **LISTENING** Music preferences / **READING** Likes and dislikes

VOCABULARY

1 Match the words with the pictures. Then listen and check your answers.

> a. pop music   c. jazz   e. dance music   g. Latin music
> b. rock music   d. electronica   f. hip-hop   h. classical music

1. _d_

2. ◯

3. ◯

4. ◯

5. ◯

6. ◯

7. ◯

8. ◯

ONLINE PRACTICE

2 **PAIR WORK.** Practice the conversation.

> What is your favorite type of music?

> My favorite type of music is _hip-hop_ . How about you?

> My favorite type of music is _____.

3 **PAIR WORK.** Complete these questions. Then ask and answer them with your partner.

1. _____ is your favorite singer?
2. _____ is your favorite band from?

24

CONVERSATION

1 Complete the conversation. Then listen and check your answers. Practice the conversation with a partner.

| a. classical music | b. Latin Sound | c. amazing | d. Latin music |

Ana Look! It's the new **1** [ ] concert!
Do you like **2** [ ]?

Alex Uh, not especially.

Ana Really? Do you like jazz?

Alex No, I don't.

Ana Huh. What kind of music do you like?

Alex I like **3** [ ]. And I like hip-hop.

Ana Me, too. Hip-hop is **4** [ ]!

Alex Well, then let's go to a hip-hop concert.

Ana Great idea!

2 **PAIR WORK.** Practice the conversation again. Use the ideas below. Add your own ideas.

1	2	3	4
Electro Haus	electronica	pop music	great
The Smarts	rock music	dance music	fantastic
_____	_____	_____	_____

CONVERSATION TIP

BEING POLITE
If you express a dislike, do it indirectly.

Do you like Latin music?

Uh, not especially.

25

LANGUAGE PRACTICE

Statements and questions with *like*		Grammar Reference page 107

I like classical music.
I don't like jazz.

Do you **like** Latin music?
What kind of music **do** you **like**?

We **like** pop music.
They **don't like** it.

Yes, **I do.**/No, **I don't.**
I like hip-hop.

Likes and dislikes
It's... amazing! ★★★★
good. ★★★☆
not bad. ★★☆☆
OK. ★☆☆☆
terrible! **X**

ONLINE PRACTICE

1 Look at the pictures. Complete the conversations. Then listen and check your answers.

1. **A** I _____like_____ hip-hop. It's
   great! How about you?
   B I __like__ electronica.

2. **A** Let's go to the Beethoven concert!
   B I _____ _____ classical
   music. It's terrible!

3. **A** What kind of music do you like?
   B I _____ jazz. It's amazing!

4. **A** I don't like _____ music.
   B Really? I _____ it.

5. **A** _____ you _____
   pop music?
   B No, I _____ _____ it.

6. **A** _____ they _____
   _____ music?
   B Yes, they _____ it.

2 PAIR WORK. Ask and answer questions about the types of music in Activity 1.

A: I <u>like</u> hip-hop. I think it's amazing. How about you?

B: I think hip-hop is <u>okay</u>.

Statements and questions with *like*—3rd person singular | Grammar Reference page 107

She **likes** Latin music.
He **doesn't like** it.

Does she **like** dance music?   Yes, she **does.**/No, she **doesn't.**
What kind of music **does** she **like**?   She **likes** jazz.

ONLINE PRACTICE

3 Complete the conversations.

1. **A** Are these your songs?
   B No, they're my brother's. He ____likes____
   classical music.
2. **A** _____ your parents _____ Latin music?
   B My father _____ it, but my mother _____
   _____ it.
3. **A** What kind of music _____ Maria _____?
   B She _____ electronica.
4. **A** _____ your sister _____ hip-hop?
   B Yes, she _____.
5. **A** Does your teacher like dance music?
   B No, he _____.

USEFUL WORDS

the guitar

the drums

the piano

the trumpet

4 PAIR WORK. Ask and answer these questions.

1. What kind of music do you not like?
2. What kind of music do your friends like?
3. What music does your teacher like?
4. What kind of music do you think is amazing?
5. What's your favorite instrument?
6. What's your parents' favorite kind of music?

PRONUNCIATION—Yes/no *question intonation*

1 Listen. Notice the rising intonation at the end of *yes/no* questions.

1. Do you like jazz?
2. Does she like dance music?

3. Are these your glasses?
4. Is this your book?

2 Listen again and repeat. Be sure to use rising intonation at the end of the questions.

LISTENING

1 BEFORE YOU LISTEN Complete the sentences with information that is true for you. Use one of the words below.

1. I think _hip-hop_ is _____ .
2. I think _____ is _____ .

1. pleasant
2. boring 
3. catchy 
4. annoying 

2 Listen to the people talking. What types of music do they like? Write the correct letter in the picture below.

a. rock music
c. classical music
b. dance music
d. Latin music

Karen

Frank

Jim c Mary

ONLINE PRACTICE

3 Listen again. Choose (✓) _True_ or _False_.

	True	False
1. Jim thinks pop music is boring.	☐	☐
2. Mary likes jazz.	☐	☐
3. Frank doesn't like dance music.	☐	☐
4. Karen thinks rock music is catchy.	☐	☐

4 Listening **PLUS**. Listen to the people later. What's their favorite type of music? Complete the chart.

Favorite type of music	
1. Jim	
2. Mary	
3. Frank	
4. Karen	

SPEAKING — *Let's go to a concert.*

1 **PAIR WORK. Look at the pictures and complete the conversation. Then practice the conversation with your partner.**

A Hi, Mike.

B Hi, Sara. Hey, let's go to the _____ concert.

A Daft Punk? I'm sorry, but I don't like _____.

B Really? I think it's amazing. Well, what type of music do you like?

A I really like _____.

B Well, let's go to a _____ concert sometime.

A That sounds fun.

2 **PAIR WORK. Look at the picture below. Role-play a conversation like the one above. How many items in the picture can you use?**

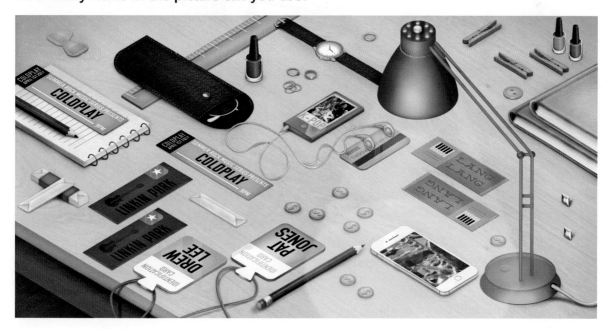

3 **PAIR WORK. Now make your own conversation. Use information that is true for you.**

GO ONLINE Find out what music is popular in a country you are interested in. Tell your classmates.

29

5 What do you do for fun?

SPEAKING Suggesting things to do	**GRAMMAR** The simple present	**LISTENING** Free time activities	**READING** What do you do for fun?

WARM UP
What do you like to do?

VOCABULARY

1 What are the people thinking about? Write the correct letter. Then listen and check your answers.

a. have coffee with friends	c. go shopping	e. play video games
b. do yoga	d. watch TV	f. listen to music

2 PAIR WORK. Practice the conversation.

A Do you like [yoga] ?
B [Not especially] . How about you?
A [I love it] !

3 PAIR WORK. Practice the conversation again. Use the ideas below. Add your own ideas.

coffee	Not especially.	Me, too.
shopping	Sometimes.	I do, too.
TV	I do.	Not really.
video games	It depends.	I'm a big fan.
_____	_____	_____

VOCABULARY TIP
Make sentences to learn new words.

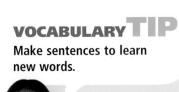

do yoga

I do yoga on Saturdays.

CONVERSATION

1 Complete the conversation. Then listen and check your answers.
Practice the conversation with a partner.

USEFUL WORDS
Monday
Tuesday
Wednesday
Thursday
Friday
Saturday
Sunday

a. rock music	b. on Friday	c. play tennis

Anthony   Ana, do you like [1   ]?
          Let's go to a concert on Saturday.
Ana   Sorry, but I'm busy.
Anthony   So, what do you do for fun?
          Do you [2   ]?
Ana   No, I don't. Sorry...
Anthony   Oh. Well, are you free [3   ]?
          Let's watch TV together.
Ana   I don't watch TV. I read books.
Anthony   OK. Hmm… Hey, do you like coffee? Let's go to a cafe.
Ana   Sorry, Anthony.

2 **PAIR WORK**. Practice the conversation again. Use the ideas below.
Add your own ideas.

1	2	3
Latin music	play soccer	tomorrow
classical music	do yoga	on Saturday
_____	_____	_____

LANGUAGE PRACTICE

The simple present—regular verbs		Grammar Reference page 108
I **play** tennis.	Do you **play** tennis?	Yes, I **do**./ No, I **don't**.
He **plays** soccer.	Where **does** he **play** soccer?	At school.
She **doesn't play** video games.		
They **don't watch** TV.		

1 Look at the pictures. Complete the conversations. Then listen and check your answers.

1. **A** Does she ___play___ tennis?
   B No, ___she___ ___doesn't___ .

2. **A** What _____ your brother do for fun?
   B He _____ to music.

3. **A** Where do you _____ _____?
   B At school.

4. **A** Where _____ Amy play games on her cell phone?
   B In class!

5. **A** _____ your sister _____ TV?
   B Yes, _____ _____.

6. **A** Where _____ Carlos and Miho _____ to music?
   B At the park.

2 PAIR WORK. Complete the following questions. Then ask and answer them with a partner.

1. Do your friends play ___soccer___?
2. Do your family members _____?

3. Do you _____?
4. Where do you _____?

The simple present—irregular verbs

Grammar Reference page 108

She **goes** shopping.
He **does** yoga.
He **has** coffee with friends.
She **doesn't do** yoga every day.

Does he **do** yoga?
When does she **do** her homework?

Yes, he **does.**/No, he **doesn't.**
On the weekend./At night.

ONLINE **PRACTICE**

3 Complete the conversations. Then practice them with a partner.

1. **A** What does Mark do for fun?
   B He ___*does*___ yoga.

2. **A** What does Tina do on the weekend?
   B She _____ shopping.

3. **A** Does Kazu listen to music every day?
   B No, he _____.

4. **A** _____ Anna _____ coffee with friends?
   B Yes, she _____.

5. **A** _____ _____ she have coffee with friends?
   B Every Sunday.

6. **A** _____ _____ they go shopping?
   B At the mall.

4 **PAIR WORK.** Complete the questions. Then ask and answer them with a partner. Use information about you.

1. What _____ you _____ for fun?
2. Do you play _____?
3. _____ your friends _____ yoga?
4. _____ _____ you _____ your homework?

PRONUNCIATION—Wh- *question intonation*

1 Listen. Notice the falling intonation at the end of *Wh-* questions.

1. Where does he play video games?
2. When does she do her homework?
3. When do they go shopping?
4. Where do you watch TV?

2 Listen again and repeat. Be sure to use falling intonation at the end of the questions.

LISTENING

1 **BEFORE YOU LISTEN** **Which of these things do you do? Check the pictures.**

1. download apps   2. send text messages   3. upload videos   4. shop online

2 **Listen to the people talking. What do they do for fun? Write the correct letter in the picture below.**

Adam and Mara

Jackie and Peter

a. surf the web   b. go shopping   c. play tennis   d. watch TV

3 **Listen again. Choose (✓) True or False.**

	True	False
1. Adam plays games on his phone.	☐	☐
2. Adam uploads videos.	☐	☐
3. Peter doesn't shop online.	☐	☐
4. Jackie goes bowling on the weekend.	☐	☐

4 **Listening PLUS. Listen to Adam and Jackie talking. When do they do these other activies? Choose the correct answer.**

1. Jackie does yoga ___.
   a. every Wednesday   b. every Friday

2. Adam goes shopping ___.
   a. every Saturday   b. every Thursday

SPEAKING — *What do you do for fun?*

1 **Read the instructions below on how to play the game.**

1. Play in pairs or groups.
2. Choose an object as a game piece.
3. Use a coin to move. Heads = 1 space. Tails = 2 spaces.
4. Take turns asking and answering questions.

> What do you do for fun?

> I play video games with friends.

2 **PAIR WORK. Now play the game. Who is the winner?**

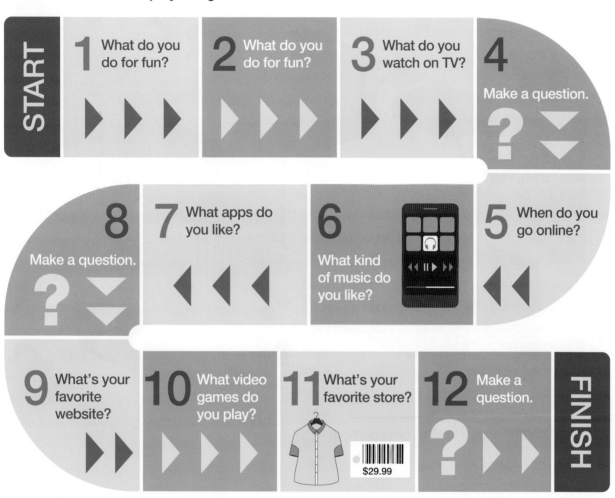

GO ONLINE Find information about what people in other countries do for fun. Tell your classmates.

NOW I CAN

SPEAKING	GRAMMAR	LISTENING	READING
☐ suggest things to do with someone.	☐ use the simple present.	☐ understand what people do in their free time.	☐ understand what people do for fun.

6 / Can you play the guitar?

SPEAKING	GRAMMAR	LISTENING	READING
Things you can do	*Can* and *can't*	Things people can do	People's abilities

WARM UP
What do you do well?

VOCABULARY

1 Match the words with the pictures. Then listen and check your answers.

a. cook	c. ride a bike	e. draw	g. play the guitar
b. dance	d. sing	f. use a computer	h. drive

ONLINE PRACTICE

2 **PAIR WORK.** Practice the conversation.

A I [cook] every day.
B Really? I [cook] on the [weekend].

3 **PAIR WORK.** Practice the conversation again. Use the ideas below. Add your own ideas.

use a computer	every day
drive	one time a week
cook	two or three times a week
_____	_____

USEFUL LANGUAGE

I rarely cook.
I never cook.

CONVERSATION

ONLINE
PRACTICE

🔊 **1** Complete the conversation. Then listen and check your answers.
Practice the conversation with a partner.

a. sing	b. French	c. drive

Ms. Smith	So, tell me, Doug, what can you do?
Doug	Well, uh, I…
Ms. Smith	Can you use a computer?
Doug	No, I can't use a computer.
Ms. Smith	I see. Can you speak 1 _____ ?
Doug	No. English is my only language.
Ms. Smith	Can you 2 _____ ?
Doug	No, not very well.
Ms. Smith	What can you do, then?
Doug	Well, I can 3 _____ very well.
Ms. Smith	OK. Well, thank you. Next!

💬 **2** **PAIR WORK.** Practice the conversation again.
Use the ideas below. Add your own ideas.

1	2	3
Korean	ride a bike	dance
Spanish	cook	play the guitar
_____	_____	_____

CONVERSATION TIP

GIVING MORE DETAILS
When you give a negative answer,
try to give extra information.

Can you speak
French?

No. English is my
only language.

37

LANGUAGE PRACTICE

Statements with *can* and *can't*	Grammar Reference page 109
I **can** sing.	**Ability**
I **can't** dance.	I **can** sing very well. ★★★★
He **can** draw.	I **can** sing well. ★★★☆
He **can't** play the guitar.	I **can** sing. ★★☆☆
They **can** play tennis.	I **can't** sing very well. ★☆☆☆
They **can't** play soccer.	I **can't** sing at all. **X**

ONLINE PRACTICE

1 Look at the pictures. Complete the sentences. Then listen and check your answers.

1. Martin ___can't___ sing.

2. Natalie and Marco _____ dance.

3. Tim _____ play the piano.

4. Ellen _____ draw.

5. Billy _____ drive _____ _____.

6. Sun-hee _____ cook _____ _____.

2 **PAIR WORK.** Can you do the things in Activity 1? Tell your partner.

> I can sing well. How about you?

> I can't sing very well.

Questions with *can*

Grammar Reference page 109

What **can** you do?	I **can** cook.
Can you play the guitar?	Yes, I **can.**/No, I **can't**.
Can he cook?	Yes, he **can**. He **can** cook very well.
Can she do yoga?	No, she **can't**, but her brother **can**.
Can they sing?	No, they **can't** sing at all.

ONLINE PRACTICE

3 Complete the conversations.

1. A ___Can___ you ___ride___ a bike?
   B No, I ___can't___ ride a bike.

2. A _____ you _____ tennis?
   B No, I _____ play at all.

3. A _____ you _____ yoga?
   B No, I can't. But my sister _____ !

4. A _____ you _____ the guitar?
   B No, I _____ .

5. A _____ you _____ ?
   B No, I _____ sing at _____ .

6. A What _____ you _____ ?
   B I _____ go shopping!

4 PAIR WORK. Look at the picture. Ask and answer questions with *can*.

Can Jinwoo cook?

Yes, he can cook very well.

Mike   Sophia   Ginger   Fred   Jinwoo

PRONUNCIATION—*Reduction of* can

1 Listen. Notice the reduced sound of *can*.

1. Can you play the guitar?   /Kən/ you play the guitar?
2. Can they play soccer?   /Kən/ they play soccer?
3. What can you do?   What /kən/ you do?
4. I can play tennis.   I /kən/ play tennis.

2 Listen again and repeat. Be sure to reduce *can*.

LISTENING

1 **BEFORE YOU LISTEN** Where do you like to relax with your friends? Check the pictures.

1. at home   **2.** at school   **3.** at a club   **4.** in the neighborhood

2 Listen to the conversations. Number the pictures below.

A.

B.

C.

D.

3 Listen again. Choose (✓) *True* or *False*.

	True	False
1. Yuko can cook very well.	☐	☐
2. Jake can't sing.	☐	☐
3. Laura can't sing.	☐	☐
4. Ben plays video games at home.	☐	☐

4 **Listening PLUS**. Listen to more of Ben's conversation. Choose the correct answer.

1. Ben can play tennis ___.   **a.** well   **b.** very well

2. He plays tennis ___.   **a.** every weekend   **b.** every day

3. Ben's parents ___ play tennis.   **a.** can   **b.** can't

SPEAKING — *Skills survey*

1 **GROUP WORK.** Find someone who can do these things. Write their names in the chart. Then ask more questions.

Can you play the piano?

Yes, I can play the piano very well.

Where do you play the piano?

I play it at home.

When do you play it?

Can You . . .	Student's Name	Can You . . .	Student's Name
1. 		5. 	
2. 		6. 	
3. 		7. 	
4. 		8. 	

2 **CLASS ACTIVITY.** What did you learn about your classmates? Share your information with the class.

Tina can play tennis. She plays it at her club on weekends.

GO ONLINE Find out some unusual abilities. Share them with the class.

NOW I CAN

SPEAKING	**GRAMMAR**	**LISTENING**	**READING**
☐ talk about things I can do.	☐ use *can/can't* to talk about abilities.	☐ understand people saying what they can do.	☐ understand phrases about what people can do.

41

1 **Read the conversation. Choose the correct answer.**

Mary	Are these your books?
Carlos	No, they aren't. They're my sister's.
Mary	Oh, so you <u>is / are</u> Lisa's brother. ̲1 Lisa is wonderful!
Carlos	Yes, she's amazing. She does yoga every morning. And she <u>play / plays</u> ̲2 music with her friends on weekends.
Mary	What kind of music does she play?
Carlos	Rock and pop music. She <u>can / does</u> ̲3 sing very well.
Mary	Can she play the piano?
Carlos	No, she can't. She plays the guitar.
Mary	<u>Can / Can't</u> you sing? ̲4
Carlos	No, I can't. And I <u>don't / doesn't</u> play ̲5 an instrument.
Mary	What <u>does / do</u> you do for fun? ̲6
Carlos	Oh, I watch TV. And I draw sometimes.

◀)) 2 **Listen and check your answers. Then practice the conversation with a partner.**

🗨 3 **PAIR WORK.** **Put a box around the activities and the kinds of music. Practice the conversation again. Use your own ideas for the activities and kinds of music.**

SMART TALK

What can they do well?	Student A: Turn to page 85. Student B: Turn to page 89.

4 Look at the pictures. How many sisters are there?

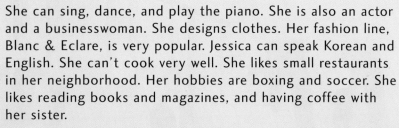

Talented Sisters

Jessica

Krystal

These are the Jung sisters.

Their names are Jessica and Krystal. They are very talented. Their hometown is San Francisco, but they live in Seoul.

This is Jessica.

She can sing, dance, and play the piano. She is also an actor and a businesswoman. She designs clothes. Her fashion line, Blanc & Eclare, is very popular. Jessica can speak Korean and English. She can't cook very well. She likes small restaurants in her neighborhood. Her hobbies are boxing and soccer. She likes reading books and magazines, and having coffee with her sister.

This is Jessica's younger sister.

Her name is Krystal. She can't play any instruments, but she can sing and dance very well. She is in the K-pop band, *f(x)*, and they sing pop and electronica music. Their songs are very catchy. Jessica's favorite kind of music is electronica. She likes the American singer Christina Aguilera. She can speak English, Korean, and Chinese. She loves to shop for clothes online. Krystal is also an actor. She acts in Korean dramas.

Jessica and Krystal have a reality TV show. What's the name of the show? *Jessica & Krystal*, of course!

5 Read the article. Choose (✓) *True* or *False*.

	True	False
1. Jessica and Krystal are sisters.	☐	☐
2. Krystal plays the piano.	☐	☐
3. Jessica can speak Chinese.	☐	☐
4. Krystal likes shopping for clothes online.	☐	☐
5. Jessica can speak another language.	☐	☐

6 GROUP WORK. What are some things can you do? Tell your group.

WRITING
Turn to page 93.

7 What's she wearing?

SPEAKING Present actions / **GRAMMAR** Present continuous / **LISTENING** What people are wearing / **READING** What people are doing

WARM UP
What are your favorite clothes?

VOCABULARY

1 Match the words with the picture. Then listen and check your answers.

a. boots	c. sneakers	e. shorts	g. a T-shirt	i. pants
b. a skirt	d. a sweater	f. jeans	h. a suit	j. sunglasses

ONLINE PRACTICE

2 **PAIR WORK.** Do you like the clothes in the picture? Tell your partner.

A I like that <u>suit</u> and those <u>jeans</u>.

B I like those <u>sunglasses</u>.

3 **PAIR WORK.** Whose clothes do you like in the class?

I like Mike's shirt. How about you?

I like Tina's sneakers.

VOCABULARY TIP
Draw pictures to learn new words.

T-shirt

44

CONVERSATION

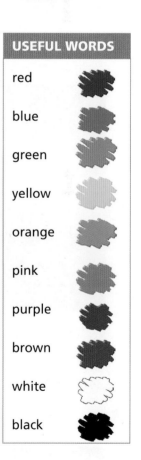

ONLINE PRACTICE

1 Complete the conversation. Then listen and check your answers. Practice the conversation with a partner.

USEFUL WORDS

a. T-shirt   b. jeans   c. drinking water

Marco	Look at that girl over there. Isn't she cute?
Alex	Which girl?
Marco	Over there. She's wearing those cool ⬚1 .
Alex	Wait. What else is she wearing?
Marco	She's wearing a ⬚2 .
Alex	OK, but I see two girls like that. What's she doing? Is she ⬚3 ?
Marco	No, she's talking on the phone.
Alex	Oh her? That's Kelly. She's my girlfriend.

USEFUL WORDS	
red	
blue	
green	
yellow	
orange	
pink	
purple	
brown	
white	
black	

2 **PAIR WORK.** Practice the conversation again. Use the ideas below. Add your own ideas.

1	2	3
pants	green shirt	dancing
boots	blue sweater	eating something
_____	_____	_____

45

LANGUAGE PRACTICE

The present continuous—statements	Grammar Reference page 110

I'm **wearing** jeans.
She**'s wearing** a T-shirt.
They**'re listening** to music.

I**'m not wearing** shorts.
She **isn't drinking** water.
They **aren't watching** TV.

ONLINE PRACTICE

1 Look at the pictures. Complete the sentences. Then listen and check your answers.

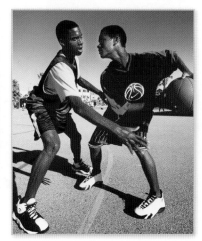

1. She's _drinking_ soda.
   She _isn't drinking_ coffee.

2. They _____ sweaters.
   They _____ T-shirts.

3. She _____ jeans.
   She _____ a dress.

4. "We _____ sneakers.
   We _____ boots."

5. "I _____ a
   hamburger.
   I _____ pizza."

6. They _____ on
   the phone.
   They _____ TV.

2 PAIR WORK. Describe what you are wearing.

I'm wearing a brown sweater,
blue jeans, and white sneakers.
I'm studying English now.

I'm wearing ___, ___, and ___.
I'm ___ now.

The present continuous—questions

Grammar Reference page 110

What's she **doing**?	She**'s dancing**.
Is she **watching** TV?	Yes, she **is**./No, she **isn't**.
What are they **doing**?	They**'re playing** video games.
Are they **talking**?	Yes, they **are**./No, they **aren't**.
What kind of shirt **is** she **wearing**?	She**'s wearing** a pink T-shirt.

ONLINE PRACTICE

3 **Match the questions and answers.**

1. What is he wearing? _b_
2. What is she doing? ___
3. Are they dancing? ___
4. What kind of music is she listening to? ___
5. Is he talking on the phone? ___
6. What are you eating? ___

a. Latin music.
b. He's wearing black pants.
c. No, they're watching TV.
d. Yes, he's talking to his sister.
e. I'm eating a hamburger.
f. She's reading a book.

4 **GROUP WORK.** Take turns miming an activity. Guess what your classmate is doing by using the present continuous.

PRONUNCIATION—*Reduced sounds in questions*

1 **Listen. Notice the reduced sounds of certain words in questions.**

Unreduced	Reduced
1. What's he doing?	*Whatsee* doing?
2. What's she doing?	*Whatshee* doing?
3. What are you doing?	*Whater* you doing?
4. What kind of music is that?	What *kinda* music is that?

2 **Listen again and repeat. Be sure to use the reduced sounds.**

LISTENING

1 **BEFORE YOU LISTEN** Match the words and the pictures.

a. casual clothes	b. business clothes	c. formal clothes	d. athletic clothes

2 Listen to people talking. Choose (✓) the correct picture.

1. a. ✓   b.   2. a.   b.

3. a.   b. ✓   4. a.   b.

3 Listen again. What are the people wearing? Choose the correct answer.

1. **a.** white sneakers   **b.** yellow sneakers
2. **a.** a blue suit   **b.** a gray suit
3. **a.** brown boots   **b.** black boots
4. **a.** black shoes   **b.** black sneakers

4 **Listening PLUS**. Listen to Isabelle and Mike later. What are they doing now?
Complete the sentences.

1. Isabelle is ___.   **a.** watching TV   **b.** cooking dinner

2. Mike is ___.   **a.** cooking dinner   **b.** having coffee

SPEAKING — *What are they doing?*

1 Look at the picture. Choose one person, but don't tell your partner.

Ted · Minhee · Ashley · Mike · Eric · Mario · Maria · Makiko · Dave

2 **PAIR WORK.** Tell your partner three things about the person. Your partner guesses. Take turns.

> She's playing soccer. She's wearing a yellow T-shirt and blue shorts.

> Is it Makiko?

> That's right!

3 **CLASS ACTIVITY.** Choose one more person with your partner. Take turns telling the class one thing about the person. Your class guesses.

> She's listening to music.

> Is it Ashley?

> No. Ashley isn't listening to music.

> It's Maria.

GO ONLINE What clothes and colors are fashionable now? Tell your class.

NOW I CAN

SPEAKING	GRAMMAR	LISTENING	READING
☐ talk about what is happening now.	☐ use the present continuous.	☐ understand what people are wearing.	☐ understand what people are doing.

49

8 | Are there any windows?

SPEAKING
Things in your home

GRAMMAR
There is and *there are*

LISTENING
Looking for things

READING
Describing rooms

WARM UP
How many rooms are in your home?

VOCABULARY

1 Match the words with the picture. Then listen and check your answers.

a. a sofa	c. chairs	e. a computer	g. a table	i. a closet
b. a bed	d. a desk	f. windows	h. curtains	j. a lamp

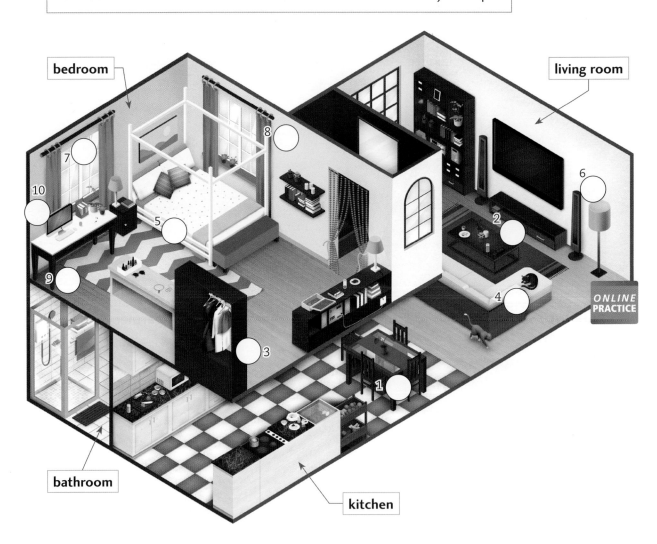

bedroom

living room

bathroom

kitchen

ONLINE PRACTICE

2 **PAIR WORK.** Look at the words again. Where are they in your home? Tell your partner.

A The <u>computer</u> is in my living room.

B The <u>desk</u> is in my bedroom.

3 **PAIR WORK.** What do you do in each room? Tell your partner.

I study in the living room.

Really? I study in the bedroom.

50

CONVERSATION

1 Complete the conversation. Then listen and check your answers.
Practice the conversation with a partner.

a. desk	b. sofa	c. nice

Clare Hi, Mom! Welcome to my new apartment!

Mom Oh, it's 1 _____.

Clare Thanks! So, let me show you around.

Mom Uh, actually…

Clare There's a 2 _____ in the living room.

Mom Clare…

Clare And there's a 3 _____ in the bedroom.

Mom Uh, Clare?

Clare Yeah, Mom?

Mom Is there a bathroom?

Clare A bathroom? Of course! I'm sorry. It's right here.

2 **PAIR WORK.** Practice the conversation again.
Use the ideas below. Add your own ideas.

1	2	3
great	chair	computer
not bad	TV	lamp
_____	_____	_____

CONVERSATION TIP

CONFIRMING INFORMATION
Repeat questions to check
information.

Is there a
bathroom?

A bathroom?

51

LANGUAGE PRACTICE

Statements with *there is* and *there are*

Grammar Reference page 111

There's a lamp behind the TV.
There are windows in the kitchen.
There isn't a computer on the desk.
There aren't any shoes under the table.

There is → There's

Prepositions of place

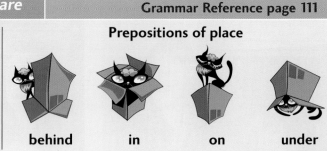

behind   in   on   under

ONLINE
PRACTICE

1 Look at the picture. Complete the sentences. Then listen and check your answers.

1. __There's__ a computer on the desk.
2. _____ pictures behind the computer.
3. _____ any books in the drawer.
4. _____ a cell phone under the desk.
5. _____ headphones on the desk.
6. _____ a bag under the desk.
7. _____ a book behind the computer.
8. _____ a lamp in the drawer.
9. _____ comic books on the chair.
10. _____ a guitar under the desk.

2 PAIR WORK. What do you see in your classroom? Tell your partner.

There are three windows.

There's a book
on my desk.

Questions with *there is* and *there are*

Grammar Reference page 111

Is there a desk in your bedroom?
Is there a computer in your living room?
Are there any chairs in your kitchen?
Are there any curtains in your living room?

Yes, **there is.**
No, **there isn't.**
Yes, **there are.**
No, **there aren't.**

ONLINE **PRACTICE**

3 **Complete the conversations.**

1. A <u> Are </u> <u> there </u> any windows
   in your kitchen?
   B No, _____ _____ .

2. A _____ _____ a TV in
   your bedroom?
   B Yes, _____ _____ .

3. A _____ _____ any chairs in
   your living room?
   B Yes, _____ _____ .

4. A _____ _____ a camera in
   your bag?
   B No, _____ _____ .

5. A _____ _____ a sofa in your
   bedroom?
   B Yes, _____ _____ .

6. A _____ _____ a lamp in
   your bathroom?
   B No, _____ _____ .

4 **PAIR WORK. Use the words to make questions. Then ask and answer them with information about you.**

1. there / cell phone / your / Is / a / bag / in
   <u> Is there a cell phone in your bag? </u>

2. computer / there / in / home / a / your / Is
   _____

3. in / sofa / living room / a / there / Is / your
   _____

4. Are / books / bedroom / in / any / there / your
   _____

Is there a cell phone in your bag?

Yes, there is. Why?

PRONUNCIATION—*Stress in content words*

1 **Listen. Notice the words that are stressed. Underline them.**

1. Is there a desk in your bedroom?
2. There's a lamp next to the bed.
3. Are there any shoes in your bag?
4. There are some books on your desk.

2 **Listen again and repeat. Be sure to stress the correct words.**

LISTENING

1 **BEFORE YOU LISTEN** **Match the words in the box with the pictures.**

| a. broken | b. brand new | c. old | d. comfortable |

2 **Listen to the conversations. Choose (✓) the correct picture.**

1. a.   b.   2. a.   b.

  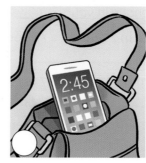 

3. a.   b.   4. a.   b.

3 **Listen again. Choose (✓) *True* or *False*.**

	True	False
1. The red sofa is in the bedroom.	☐	☐
2. There aren't any headphones in the kitchen.	☐	☐
3. There's a broken computer in John's apartment.	☐	☐
4. There's a cell phone in the bedroom.	☐	☐

4 **Listening PLUS. Listen to more of the conversations. What other things do the people ask about? Where are they? Complete the sentences.**

1. The wallet is in the kitchen, <u>under the table</u>.
2. The English book is on the sofa, _____.
3. The glasses are in the _____.
4. The sweater is in the kitchen, _____.

SPEAKING — *What's in your room?*

1 Make a list of the things in your room. Try to describe them.

You	Your Partner
There's a comfortable bed.	
There's an old lamp.	

2 **PAIR WORK.** Compare answers with your partner. Complete the chart with your partner's information. Ask your partner follow-up questions.

> There's a computer in my room.

> Where is it?

> It's on my desk.

> Is it new?

> No, it's old.

3 **CLASS ACTIVITY.** Tell the class about the things in your room and in your partner's room.

> There's a computer in Sara's room. It's not new. It's old.

GO ONLINE Find out about different styles of houses and apartments in different countries. Tell your class what you found out.

NOW I CAN

SPEAKING	GRAMMAR	LISTENING	READING
☐ describe what is in my home.	☐ use *there is* and *there are*.	☐ understand where things are in a home.	☐ understand short descriptions of rooms.

9 / The bank is on the corner.

SPEAKING / **GRAMMAR** / **LISTENING** / **READING**
Directions in a town / Places and directions / Following directions / Directions

WARM UP
What's in your neighborhood?

VOCABULARY

1 Match the words with the pictures. Then listen and check your answers.

a. drugstore	d. bank	g. department store
b. subway station	e. public restrooms	h. park
c. post office	f. traffic light	i. convenience store

ONLINE PRACTICE

2 **PAIR WORK.** Practice the conversation.

A Where do you usually [hang out with your friends]?
B [At a coffee shop.] How about you?
A [Online!]

3 **PAIR WORK.** Practice the conversation again. Use the ideas below. Add your own ideas.

have lunch	in the park
buy clothes	at a department store
study	at home
_____	_____

VOCABULARY TIP
Make a word-of-the-day calendar. Use the word three times during the day.

January 23
convenience store

CONVERSATION

ONLINE PRACTICE

1 Complete the conversation. Then listen and check your answers. Practice the conversation with a partner.

| a. drugstore | b. department store | c. subway station |

Man   Excuse me. Where's the
          [1]?
Kelly It's on Center Street.
Man   On Center Street?
Kelly Yes. It's next to the
          [2]. Go straight on
          Main Street and turn right on Center
          Street.
Man   Go straight on Main. Turn right
          on Center.
Kelly That's right. It's across from the [3].
Man   Thanks a lot!
Kelly You're welcome.

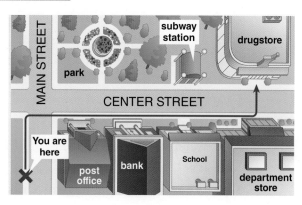

2 PAIR WORK. Practice the conversation again. Use the ideas below. Add your own ideas.

1	2	3
bank	post office	park
convenience store	bank	subway station
_____	_____	_____

LANGUAGE PRACTICE

Prepositions of place   Grammar Reference page 112

The park is **on** Pine Street.
It's **across from** the subway station.
It's **next to** the school.

It's **on the corner of** Pine and Elm.
It's **between** the school **and** the bank.

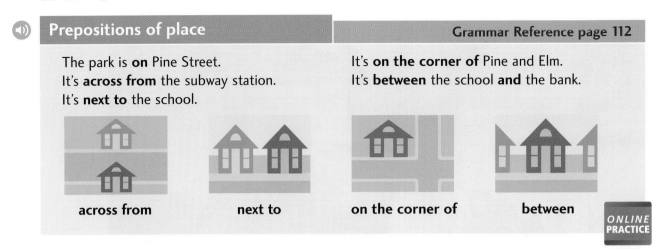

across from   next to   on the corner of   between

ONLINE PRACTICE

1 Look at the map. Complete the conversations. Then listen and check your answers.

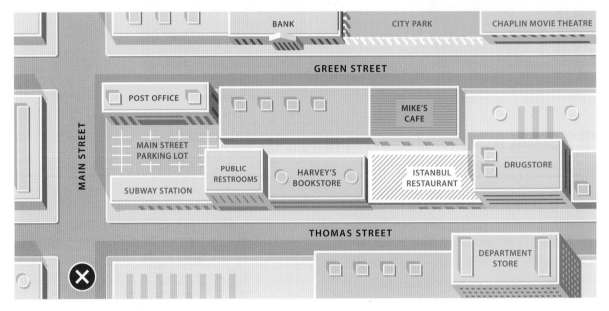

1. A Where's the bank?
   B It's _____on_____ Green Street.
2. A Where's the post office?
   B It's _____ _____ _____ _____ Main and Green.
3. A Where are the public restrooms?
   B They're _____ _____ the subway station.
4. A Where's the drugstore?
   B It's _____ _____ the department store.

2 **PAIR WORK.** Practice the conversation again. Ask and answer about other places on the map.

Where's Istanbul Restaurant?

It's on _____.

Giving directions

Grammar Reference page 112

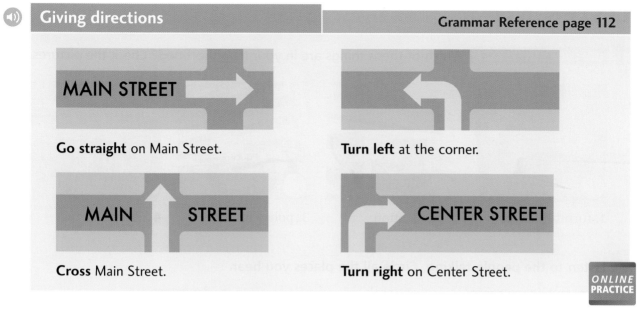

Go straight on Main Street.

Turn left at the corner.

Cross Main Street.

Turn right on Center Street.

ONLINE
PRACTICE

3 Complete the conversations and use the map on page 58. Then listen and check your answers.

1. A Where's the bank?

   B ___Go___ ___straight___ on Main Street and _____ Green Street.
   It's next to the park.

2. A Excuse me. Is there a bookstore near here?

   B Yes. Go straight on _____ Steet and turn right on _____ Street.
   It's between the public restrooms and the restaurant.

3. A Where's the park?

   B Go straight on Thomas Street and _____ _____ on Main Street.
   Then _____ _____ on Green Street. It's next to the movie theater.

4. A Is there a subway station near here?

   B Yes, there is. _____ _____ on Main Street.
   It's on the corner of Main Street and _____ Street.

4 **PAIR WORK.** Practice the conversations with a partner.
Take turns asking and answering the questions.

PRONUNCIATION—*Rising intonation for confirmation*

1 Listen. Notice the rising intonation when words are repeated for confirmation.

1. A It's across from the bank.

   B Across from the bank?

2. A The store is next to the station.

   B Next to the station?

2 Listen again and repeat. Be sure to use rising intonation when asking for confirmation.

LISTENING

1 BEFORE YOU LISTEN Which of these things are in your neighborhood? Check the pictures.

1. furniture store   2. gas station   3. police station   4. library

2 Listen to the people talking. Circle all the places you hear.

1. a. public restrooms   b. park   c. drugstore
2. a. subway station   b. furniture store   c. library
3. a. park   b. convenience store   c. gas station
4. a. library   b. post office   c. police station

3 Listen again. Where are the places below? Write the numbers on the map.

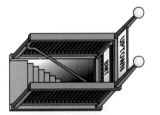  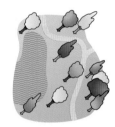 

1. subway station   2. post office   3. park   4. gas station

4 Listening PLUS. Listen to the man asking for directions. Choose (✓) *True* or *False*.

	True	False
1. There are public restrooms in the furniture store.	☐	☐
2. There are public restrooms in the convenience store.	☐	☐
3. There are public restrooms next to the park.	☐	☐
4. The park is on Smith Street.	☐	☐

SPEAKING — *What's in your neighborhood?*

1 Draw a map of the area around where you live. Draw the places and write the street names. Then draw an **X**.

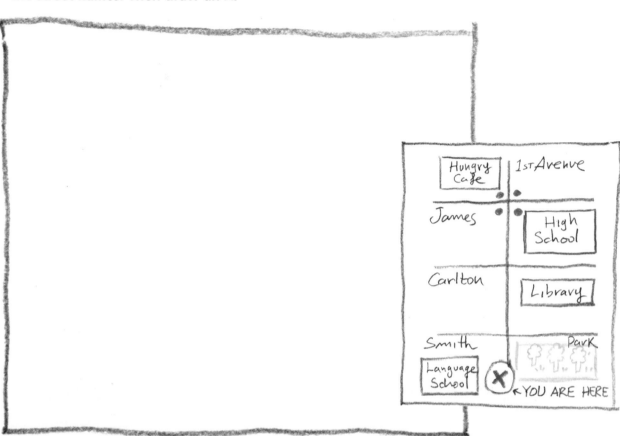

2 **PAIR WORK.** Take turns asking directions to places on your map. Start from the **X**.

Is there *a coffee shop* **around here?**

Yes, the Hungry Café is good. It's on...Street.

Excuse me. Can you repeat that?

Yes, there's one next to the _____.

3 **GROUP WORK.** Take turns giving directions to a place near your school. Your group guesses the place.

GO ONLINE Find a map of a city you want to visit. What are some places you see on the map? Tell your class.

NOW I CAN

SPEAKING	GRAMMAR	LISTENING	READING
☐ give and follow short, simple directions.	☐ describe locations and give directions.	☐ listen and follow directions on a map.	☐ understand directions on a map.

1 Read the conversation. Choose the correct answer.

Paula	Hi, Emily.
Emily	Hi, Paula. Where are you?
Paula	I'm *on / under* Main Street, at Mike's ⎵ 1 Restaurant.
Emily	What are you doing there?
Paula	I'm *eat / eating* a hamburger. How ⎵ 2 about you?
Emily	I'm watching TV at home. Hey, do you want to go shopping?
Paula	Sure. *Are there / Is there* a department ⎵ 3 store near here?
Emily	Yes. There's one on Green Street.
Paula	Really? Where on Green Street?
Emily	It's *between / on* the post office and ⎵ 4 the bank.
Paula	Is there a bank on Green Street?
Emily	Yes, there is. It's *next to / next from* the ⎵ 5 subway station.
Paula	OK. Let's meet at the department store at 3 o'clock.
Emily	Great! See you soon.

🔊 **2** Listen and check your answers. Then practice the conversation with a partner.

🗩 **3** **PAIR WORK.** Put a box around the places. Practice the conversation again. Use your own ideas for the places.

SMART TALK

Where's the subway station?   Student A: Turn to page 86.
Student B: Turn to page 90.

4 Look at the pictures. What do you see?

To: carlos@webmail.com

Subject: What's Up?

Hi, Carlos!

Hello from Miami Beach! It's really great here. The weather is amazing! What do you think of my photos? I'm wearing my new sunglasses in the first photo. There are good stores in Miami. I go shopping every day!

I really like the hotel, too. My room is great. There's a comfortable bed, a desk, and two chairs. There isn't a sofa, but there's a big window. I'm sitting at the desk writing to you now!

The beach is across from the hotel. Actually, the beach isn't so good. It's very crowded. I usually go to the hotel pool.

How's the weather in Chicago? See you soon!

Min-ji

---

5 Read the email. Answer the questions.

1. Where is Min-ji?
2. Where is Carlos?
3. What does Min-ji do every day?
4. What's in her hotel room?
5. Where is the beach?

6 GROUP WORK. Think of a place that you like. Where is it? What do you do there? Tell your group.

WRITING

Turn to page 94.

VOCABULARY

1 Match the words with the picture. Then listen and check your answers.

a. rice	e. ice cream	i. bananas	m. coffee
b. apples	f. chicken	j. potatoes	n. milk
c. fish	g. bread	k. cake	o. tea
d. cookies	h. lettuce	l. pasta	p. juice

2 PAIR WORK. Do you like the foods above? Tell your partner.

A I like <u>rice</u>, <u>fish</u>, and <u>pasta</u>. How about you?

B I like <u>cake</u>, <u>cookies</u>, and <u>ice cream</u>.

3 PAIR WORK. What do you usually eat and drink?
Ask and answer questions. Use the expressions in the box.

What do you usually have for <u>breakfast</u>**?**

Usually, I have <u>coffee and bread</u>**.
How about you?**

USEFUL WORDS

breakfast
lunch
dinner

CONVERSATION

ONLINE
PRACTICE

🔊 **1** **Complete the conversation. Then listen and check your answers.**
Practice the conversation with a partner.

| a. bananas | b. milk | c. orange juice |

Doug Oh, no! We don't have any food.

Clare Do you want to go shopping?

Doug I can't. I have to work tonight.

Clare Well, I'm not busy. I can go.

Doug Really? Great. We need some [1 _____]. We don't have any.

Clare OK. I can buy some. What else do we need?

Doug We need some [2 _____].

Clare Yes, and we don't have any [3 _____], either.

Doug Yes, we do. They're on the stove!

2 **PAIR WORK. Practice the conversation again.**
Use the ideas below. Add your own ideas.

1	2	3
chicken	bread	cookies
fish	rice	potatoes
_____	_____	_____

CONVERSATION TIP

BEING POLITE
If you refuse a request, give
a reason.

Do you want to go
shopping?

I can't. I have to
work tonight.

65

LANGUAGE PRACTICE

Count and noncount nouns   Grammar Reference page 113

Count nouns
There's **an apple**.
There are **two potatoes**.
There are **some potatoes**.

Noncount nouns
There's **some lettuce**.
There's **some juice,** too.

ONLINE PRACTICE

1 Complete the sentences. Choose the correct answers. Then listen and check your answers.

1. There's a / some coffee on the table.

2. Here's a / some cookie for you.

3. There's a / some chicken on the plate.

4. I have a / five potatoes.

5. I have a / some pasta for dinner.

6. I think there's a / some bread in the kitchen.

7. There's an / some apple on the table.

8. We need a / some milk.

9. I think there are a / some bananas in the kitchen.

2 PAIR WORK. Take turns describing what you see in the shopping basket.

There is some fish.

There is a banana.

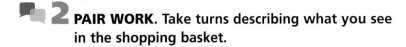

Some and *any*

Grammar Reference page 113

Some
We have **some** cake.
We have **some** bananas.

Any
There isn't **any** milk.
There aren't **any** cookies.

Are there **any** bananas?
  Yes, there are.

Do we have **any** milk?
  No, we don't.

ONLINE PRACTICE

3 **Complete the conversations. Use *some* or *any*.**

1. **A** I'm going to the store. Do we have ___any___ milk?
   B Yes, we have ___some___ in the refrigerator.

2. **A** Do you want a snack? I have _____ cookies and _____ milk.
   B No, thanks. I'm not hungry.

3. **A** Do we have _____ lettuce?
   B No, we don't, but I can buy _____.

4. **A** Do we have _____ fruit?
   B We don't have _____ apples, but there are _____ bananas on the table.

4 **PAIR WORK. Look at the words in the box. Which food and drinks do you have at home? Ask and answer questions.**

A I have some <u>tea</u> and some <u>milk</u>.
B Do you have any <u>coffee</u>?
A No, I don't, but I have some <u>juice</u>. How about you?
B I have some <u>ice cream</u> and <u>two</u> <u>bananas</u>.

tea	chicken	juice
milk	fish	rice
coffee	ice cream	bread
potatoes	cake	bananas
lettuce		

PRONUNCIATION—*Intonation for items in a series*

1 **Listen. Notice the different intonation when words are said in a series.**

1. We have some coffee, some tea, and some juice.

2. There's some bread, some cake, and some rice.

3. I need to get some apples, some potatoes, and some fish.

2 **Listen again and repeat. Be sure to change your intonation.**

LISTENING

1 **BEFORE YOU LISTEN** **Match the words in the box with the pictures.**

| a. a medium pizza | b. a small pizza | c. a slice of pizza | d. a large pizza |

1.

2.

3.

4.

2 **Listen to the people talking. Number the recipes.**

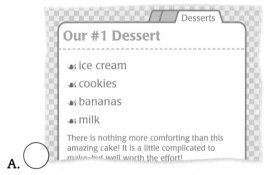

Desserts

Our #1 Dessert

- ice cream
- cookies
- bananas
- milk

There is nothing more comforting than this amazing cake! It is a little complicated to make—but well worth the effort!

A. ◯

The MONSTER Sandwich

★ bread   ★ chicken

★ lettuce   ★ apples

This could quite possibly be the most delicious sandwich you'll ever

B. ◯

Auntie's INDIAN DINNER

❖ chicken
❖ potatoes
❖ rice
❖ fish

Wash and peel the potatoes. Next, thinly slice the potatoes, cover and set aside. In a large pot, place about 3 tablespoons of cooking oil and

C. ◯

POWER FRUIT DRINK

▸ milk
▸ juice
▸ a large banana
▸ 3 apples

D. ①

3 **Listen again. What things *don't* they have? Circle the correct answer.**

1. a. some milk   b. three apples   c. one large banana
2. a. some chicken   b. some bread   c. some lettuce
3. a. potatoes, chicken, and rice   b. potatoes, chicken, and fish   c. fish and rice
4. a. cookies, bananas, and milk   b. cookies and ice cream   c. ice cream and milk

4 **Listening PLUS. Listen to more of the last conversation. Choose (✓) *True* or *False*.**

	True	False
1. The woman wants a large pizza for dinner.	☐	☐
2. The man doesn't like Indian food.	☐	☐
3. They have some apples.	☐	☐
4. They make the Monster Sandwich.	☐	☐

SPEAKING — *Do you want some milk?*

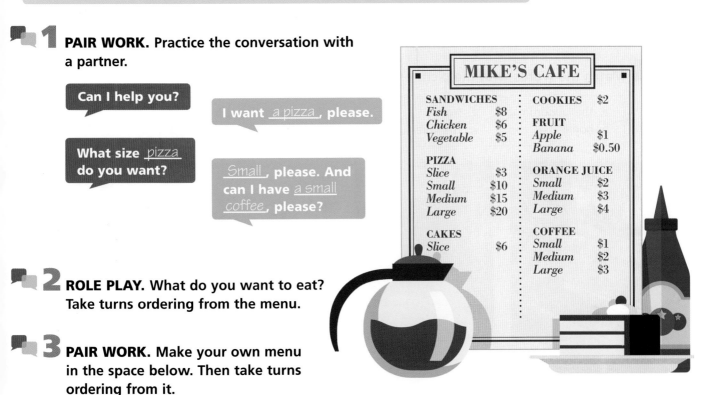

1 **PAIR WORK.** Practice the conversation with a partner.

> Can I help you?

> I want _a pizza_, please.

> What size _pizza_ do you want?

> _Small_, please. And can I have _a small coffee_, please?

MIKE'S CAFE

SANDWICHES		COOKIES	$2
Fish	$8		
Chicken	$6	**FRUIT**	
Vegetable	$5	Apple	$1
		Banana	$0.50
PIZZA			
Slice	$3	**ORANGE JUICE**	
Small	$10	Small	$2
Medium	$15	Medium	$3
Large	$20	Large	$4
CAKES		**COFFEE**	
Slice	$6	Small	$1
		Medium	$2
		Large	$3

2 **ROLE PLAY.** What do you want to eat? Take turns ordering from the menu.

3 **PAIR WORK.** Make your own menu in the space below. Then take turns ordering from it.

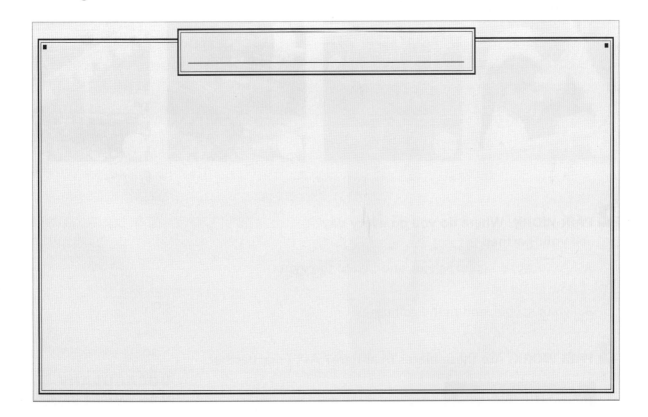

GO ONLINE Find out how much your favorite food costs in three countries you want to visit. Tell your class.

NOW I CAN

SPEAKING	GRAMMAR	LISTENING	READING
☐ talk about food and drink.	☐ use count/noncount nouns and *some/any*.	☐ understand what is needed to make recipes.	☐ understand phrases about food and drinks.

11 Where were you yesterday?

| SPEAKING Where you were | GRAMMAR Past tense of *be* | LISTENING Where people were | READING Past activities and places |

WARM UP
When do you go to the supermarket?

VOCABULARY

1 Match the words with the pictures. Then listen and check your answers.

| a. the laundromat | c. work | e. school | g. the mall |
| b. home | d. the library | f. the gym | h. the supermarket |

1.

2.

3.

4.

5.

6.

7.

8.

ONLINE PRACTICE

2 PAIR WORK. Where do you go every day?
Tell your partner.

A I go to <u>work</u>, I go to <u>school</u>, and I go to <u>the gym</u>.
How about you?

B I go to <u>school</u>, and then I go <u>home</u>.

3 PAIR WORK. Are these places near here? Ask your partner.

> Excuse me. Is there <u>a gym</u> near here?

> Yes, there is. It's <u>on Center Steet, next to the post office.</u>

VOCABULARY TIP
Make sentences using new words.

the gym

I go to <u>the gym</u> every day.

CONVERSATION

ONLINE PRACTICE

1 Complete the conversation. Then listen and check your answers. Practice the conversation with a partner.

a. home	b. laundromat	c. school

Mom   Chris, your room is still messy! It's your job to clean it.

Chris   Sorry, Mom. I was really busy.

Mom   Oh, really? So, where were you all day?

Chris   I was at 1 [_____] this morning. Then I was at the 2 [_____] And I was at the supermarket, too.

Mom   I don't believe you. Were you at 3 [_____] all day?

Chris   No, I wasn't! Really! I was just at the supermarket.

Mom   Well, I was just there. But *you* weren't.

Chris   Oh, umm... Sorry, Mom.

2 **PAIR WORK.** Practice the conversation again. Use the ideas below. Add your own ideas.

1	2	3
work	library	the mall
the gym	bank	the park
_____	_____	_____

71

LANGUAGE PRACTICE

Past tense statements with *be*

Grammar Reference page 114

He **was** at home.
She **was** at the supermarket.
I **was** at home.

I **wasn't** at the gym.
was not → wasn't

We **were** at school.
You **were** at the mall all day.
They **were** at the library.

They **weren't** at home.
were not → weren't

at home/at school/at work
at the mall/at the park

1 Look at the pictures. Where were the people? Complete the sentences. Then listen and check your answers.

1. Kelly and Mike ___were___ at the mall yesterday. It ___was___ great!

2. Lily and Seth _____ at the gym this morning. It _____ good.

3. Last weekend, Sun-hee _____ at home. It _____ OK.

4. Dave _____ at the laundromat last night. It _____ awful!

2 **PAIR WORK. Choose one of the times in the box. Ask your partner where they were at that time.**

9:00 a.m. yesterday	6:00 p.m. yesterday
10:00 p.m. yesterday	1:00 a.m. today

Where were you at 9:00 a.m. yesterday?

I was at _____.

Past tense questions with *be*

Grammar Reference page 114

Were you here this morning?	Yes, I **was**./No, I **wasn't**.
Was he at work yesterday?	Yes, he **was**./No, he **wasn't**.
Were they at school yesterday?	Yes, they **were**./No, they **weren't**.
Where **were** you all day?	I **was** at the library.
Where **was** she last night?	She **was** at work.
How **was** your day?	It **was** great/good/OK/awful.

ONLINE PRACTICE

3 Complete the conversations.

1. A How ___was___ your day?
   B It _____ awful.
   A Really? Where _____ you?
   B I _____ at work!

2. A _____ they at school today?
   B No, they _____.
   A Where _____ they?
   B They _____ at the mall.

3. A Where _____ Kevin last night?
   B He _____ at the library.
   A _____ you at the library, too?
   B No, I _____. I _____ at the gym.

4. A Where _____ you this morning?
   B I _____ at the gym.
   A _____ Mari there, too?
   B Yes, she _____.

4 PAIR WORK. Answer the questions with information about you.
Then ask and answer the questions with a partner.

1. Where were you last night?
   _____ I was at the library. _____

2. Where were you this morning?
   _____

3. Were you at school yesterday?
   _____

4. Were you at work today?
   _____

Where were you last night?

I was at the library.

PRONUNCIATION—*Reduction of sounds with* was

1 Listen. Notice the reduced sounds before *was*.

Unreduced	Reduced
1. How was your day?	*Howuhz* your day?
2. It was great.	*Ihwuhz* great.
3. It was awful.	*Ihwuhz* awful.

2 Listen again and repeat. Be sure to reduce the sounds before *was*.

LISTENING

1 **Match the words and the pictures.**

a. busy	b. sick	c. bored	d. tired

1.   2.   3.   4.

2 **Listen to the people talking. Where were they yesterday? Number the pictures.**

A.

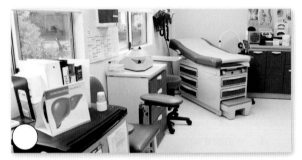

B.

C.

D.

3 **Listen again. Choose (✓) True or False.**

	True	False
1. Suzie was sick on Monday.	☐	☐
2. Andy was at the library on the weekend.	☐	☐
3. Tina wasn't at work on Thursday.	☐	☐
4. Mark was bored at the gym this morning.	☐	☐

4 **Listening PLUS. Listen to more of the conversations. Complete the sentences.**

1. Suzie was at _____ on Saturday.
2. Andy was at _____ on his birthday.
3. Tina was at _____ on Sunday.
4. Mark was at _____ yesterday morning.

SPEAKING — *Class Survey*

1 GROUP WORK. Find someone who was in one of these places yesterday. Write their names in the chart. Then ask for more information.

A Were you at <u>the gym</u> yesterday?

B Let me see. Yes, I was.

A Where is your gym?

B It's on Main Street, next to the library.

A Were you at <u>the park</u> yesterday?

B No, I was at work.

A Were you busy?

B Yes, I was really busy!

Places	Student's Name
1. the gym	
2. the bank	
3. the laundromat	
4. a bookstore	
5. the park	
6. a movie theater	
7. the library	
8. work	

2 CLASS ACTIVITY. What did you learn about your classmates? Share your information with the class.

> **Kristine was at the gym yesterday. Her gym is next to the library.**

GO ONLINE Find out the most popular places where you live. Tell your classmates where they are.

NOW I CAN

SPEAKING	GRAMMAR	LISTENING	READING
☐ talk about where I was.	☐ use the past tense of *be*.	☐ understand where people were.	☐ understand where people were last week.

75

12 What did you do?

SPEAKING	GRAMMAR	LISTENING	READING
Past activities	Simple past	Weekend activities	Past activities

VOCABULARY

1 Match the words with the pictures. Then listen and check your answers.

a. see a movie	c. do my homework	e. go to a party	g. take a trip
b. visit family	d. hang out with friends	f. clean my room	h. stay home

2 **PAIR WORK.** What do you do on weekends? Tell your partner.

A I <u>visit family</u> on weekends. What about you?

B I <u>stay home</u>!

3 **PAIR WORK.** How often do you do the things above?
Tell your partner.

I _sometimes_ stay home.
How about you?

I _always_ go out!
I'm bored at home.

USEFUL WORDS
never
rarely
sometimes
often
always

ONLINE PRACTICE

76

CONVERSATION

ONLINE
PRACTICE

1 Complete the conversation. Then listen and check your answers.
Practice the conversation with a partner.

| a. to a party | b. math | c. pretty good | d. sister |

Marco   So, Ana, did you have a good weekend?
Ana   Yeah, it was 1 _____. And you?
Marco   My weekend wasn't bad. So, what did you do?
Ana   Well, I saw a movie with my 2 _____ on Friday night.
        And on Saturday morning, I stayed home.
Marco   What did you do on Saturday night?
Ana   Oh, I hung out with friends.
Marco   Did you go 3 _____?
Ana   No, we didn't. We saw another movie.
Marco   So, when did you do your 4 _____
        homework?
Ana   Homework? Oh, no! I was so busy, I forgot!

2 **PAIR WORK.** Practice the conversation again.
Use the ideas below. Add your own ideas.

1	2	3	4
amazing	friend	to the beach	English
OK	brother	shopping	economics
_____	_____	_____	_____

CONVERSATION TIP

TURN-TAKING
Follow your answer to a question
by asking the same question.

Did you have a
good weekend?

It was pretty
good. And you?

77

LANGUAGE PRACTICE

The simple past—statements

Grammar Reference page 115

Regular verbs
I **stayed** home.
He **cleaned** his room.

They **visited** family.
They **didn't visit** friends.

Irregular verbs
I **went** to a party.
We **saw** a movie.

She **did** the laundry.
She **didn't do** her homework.

Present	Past
do	did
forget	forgot
go	went
hang out	hung out
have	had
see	saw
take	took

ONLINE PRACTICE

1 Look at the pictures. Complete the sentences. Then listen and check your answers.

1. Eun-mi _saw a movie_ on Friday night.

2. She _____ on Saturday morning.

3. Eun-mi and her friends _____ on Saturday afternoon.

4. They _____ on Saturday night.

5. Eun-mi _____ on Sunday.

6. She _____ her room.

2 PAIR WORK. Tell your partner three things you did last weekend.

> I stayed home. I cooked dinner. I watched TV. How about you?

The simple past—questions	Grammar Reference page 115
Did you **have** a good weekend? **Did** she **go** to a party? What **did** you **do** on Saturday night? Where **did** he **go** last summer? When **did** they **see** a movie?	Yes, I **did**./No, I **didn't**. Yes, she **did**./No, she **didn't**. I **hung out** with friends. He **went** to the beach. They **saw** one on Saturday night.

ONLINE PRACTICE

3 Complete the conversations.

1. A Did you have a good weekend?
   B Yes, I _____.
   A What _____ you _____?
   B I _____ to a party. How about you?
   A I _____ a trip with my parents.

2. A _____ you _____ a good weekend?
   B No, I _____. I _____ home and _____ my room.
   A _____ you _____ anything else?
   B Yeah, I also _____ a bad movie.

4 **PAIR WORK. Use the words to make questions. Then ask and answer them with information about you.**

1. go / did / you / Where / this / weekend
   <u>Where did you go this weekend</u>?
2. your / When / did / room / clean / you
   _____?
3. visit / When / you / family / did / your
   _____?
4. you / do / did / on / Monday / What
   _____?

Where did you go this weekend?

I went to the beach.

PRONUNCIATION—*Reduction of* did you

1 Listen. Notice the reduced sounds of *did you*.

Unreduced	Reduced
1. Did you stay home?	*Diju* stay home?
2. Did you take a trip?	*Diju* take a trip?
3. Where did you go?	Where *diju* go?
4. What did you do?	*Whadiju* do?

2 Listen again and repeat. Be sure to reduce *did you*.

LISTENING

1 BEFORE YOU LISTEN **Match the words and the pictures.**

a. interesting   b. crowded   c. sad   d. noisy

1.

2.

3.

4.

2 **Listen to the people talking about their weekend. Number the pictures.**

A.

B.

C.

D.

3 **Listen again. Choose (✓) *True* or *False*.**

	True	False
1. Kate went to New York with her friend.	☐	☐
2. Dave took an interesting trip with Linda.	☐	☐
3. Angela had fun at the supermarket.	☐	☐
4. Bob went to a noisy restaurant.	☐	☐

4 **Listening PLUS. Listen to more of the conversations. What else did the people do? Choose the correct answer.**

1. Kate ___.
   a. visited family
   b. stayed home
   c. saw a movie

2. Dave and Linda ___.
   a. stayed home
   b. went to a party
   c. hung out with friends

3. Angela ___.
   a. did her homework
   b. did the laundry
   c. went to work

4. Bob ___.
   a. went to the mall
   b. did his homework
   c. cleaned his room

SPEAKING — *What did you do recently?*

1 **Read the instructions below on how to play the game.**

1. Play in pairs or groups.
2. Choose a marker.
3. Use a coin to move. Heads = 1 space. Tails= 2 spaces.
4. Take turns asking and answering questions.

> **What did you have for breakfast today?**

> **I had some rice and some fish.**

2 **PAIR WORK. Now play the game. Who is the winner?**

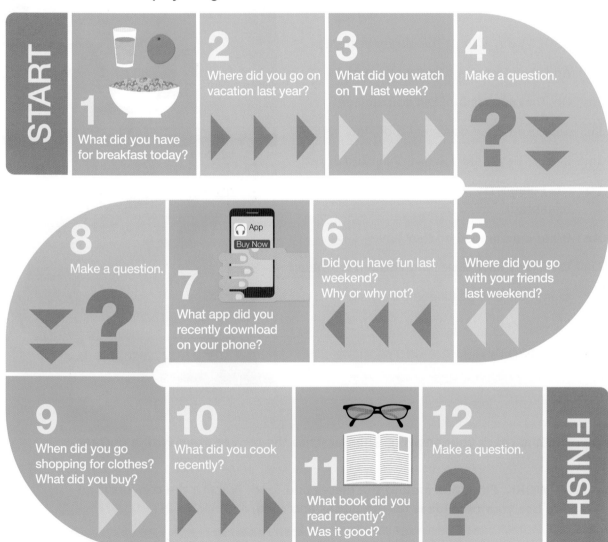

GO ONLINE Find interesting events or things to do on the weekend. Tell your classmates.

NOW I CAN

SPEAKING	GRAMMAR	LISTENING	READING
☐ talk about past activities.	☐ use the simple past tense.	☐ understand past weekend activities.	☐ understand phrases about past activities.

1 **Read the conversation. Choose the correct answer.**

Liz   Hey, Kim! Wow, you have a lot of bags.
Where <u>were / was</u> you today?
₁

Kim   Oh, hi, Liz! Yeah, I was really busy today.
I went to the mall and the supermarket.

Liz   Really? I went to the supermarket
yesterday. This morning I <u>went / go</u> to the
₂
laundromat. Here, let me help you.

Kim   Oh, thanks! Did you do anything else this
weekend?

Liz   Yeah, I <u>was / were</u> at the library yesterday.
₃
And then last night I went to a party.

Kim   Oh, that sounds fun! Did you dance?

Liz   Sure! And there was great food, too.

Kim   Really? Hey… did you <u>had / have</u> lunch yet?
₄

Liz   No, I didn't. Do you want to eat at this
restaurant?

Kim   What kind of food do they have?

Liz   Well, they have <u>some / any</u> chicken on the
₅
menu. Oh, and pasta and pizza, too!

Kim   I love pasta!

Liz   Me, too. Let's eat!

2 **Listen and check your answers. Then practice the conversation with a partner.**

3 **PAIR WORK. Put a box around the places and food. Practice the conversation again. Use your own ideas for the places and food.**

SMART TALK

| *What did they do?* | Student A: Turn to page 87.
Student B: Turn to page 91. |

4 Look at the article and the pictures. What do you think *spring break* means?

Spring Break
An American Tradition

In March many college students in the US go on vacation for a week. It's called *spring break*. Many students go to the beach in Florida, Texas, or Mexico. Let's find out where these students went.

> "Where did you go for spring break?"

Linda Porter
Age 21
California State University

"My friends went to Mexico, but I stayed home. I wanted to go, but I had too much homework. I didn't have any money, either. I was at the library at school every day."

Brian Chan
Age 19
Duke University

"I'm from Canada. I visited my family in Toronto. We stayed home, watched TV, and saw movies. It was OK."

Carla Lewis
Age 20
New York University

"I had a great time! My sister and I took a trip to Florida. We went to the beach every day. I wore my new sunglasses! At night, we went to parties. The food was really good. We had some great fruit and juice at breakfast. We had some amazing fish for dinner, too."

5 Read the article and answer the questions.

1. When is spring break?
2. Where do many students go for spring break?
3. What did Linda do for spring break?
4. Where did Brian go this year?
5. What did Carla do in Florida?

6 GROUP WORK. Did you take a trip with your school, your family, or your friends? Where did you go? Tell your group.

WRITING
Turn to page 95.

UNITS 1–3 *What's his phone number?*
Student A

1 **PAIR WORK. Ask and answer questions to complete the information.**

A What's <u>Mike's</u> phone number?

B His phone number is <u>749-6345</u>. What's <u>his</u> email address?

A <u>His</u> email address is <u>mike@net.com</u>.

1. **Name:** Mike Johnson
   Phone: <u>749-6345</u>
   Email: mike@net.com
   Job: programmer
   Hobby: _____

2. **Name:** Julia Rivera
   Phone: _____
   Email: jrivera@hi.com
   Job: engineer
   Hobby: _____

3. **Name:** Amy Hooper
   Phone: _____
   Email: ahoop@my.net
   Job: _____
   Hobby: swimming

4. **Name:** Richard Wong
   Phone: 381-1408
   Email: _____
   Job: teacher
   Hobby: _____

2 **Ask about your partner. Complete the sentences.**

1. My partner's name is _____.
2. His/Her phone number is _____.
3. His/Her email address is _____.
4. His/Her mother's name is _____.
5. His/Her father's name is _____.
6. His/Her hobby is _____.

> What's your ... ?

> What's your mother's ... ?

> What's your father's ... ?

UNITS 4–6 *What can they do well?*
Student A

1 **PAIR WORK. Ask and answer questions to complete the chart.**

A What can <u>Alan</u> do very well?
B He can <u>speak Chinese</u> very well. What can he do well?
A He can <u>play the piano</u> well. What *can't* he do?
B He can't <u>do yoga</u> at all.

	Very well	Well	Not at all
Alan	speak Chinese	play the piano	do yoga
Meg	dance		play tennis
Kazu and Hiro		play video games	
Jen	sing		draw

2 **Ask and answer questions to complete the sentences.**

1. My partner can _____ well.
2. My partner can _____ very well.
3. My partner can't _____ at all.
4. My partner's friends can _____ well.
5. My partner's friends can't _____ at all.

> **What can you do ... ?**

> **What can your friends do ... ?**

85

UNITS 7–9 *Where's the subway station?*
Student A

1 **PAIR WORK. Ask and answer questions to complete the map. Ask about the places in the box.**

| subway station | library | shopping mall | drugstore |

A Where's the <u>subway station</u>?

B It's on <u>Center Street</u>. It's <u>across from the park</u>.

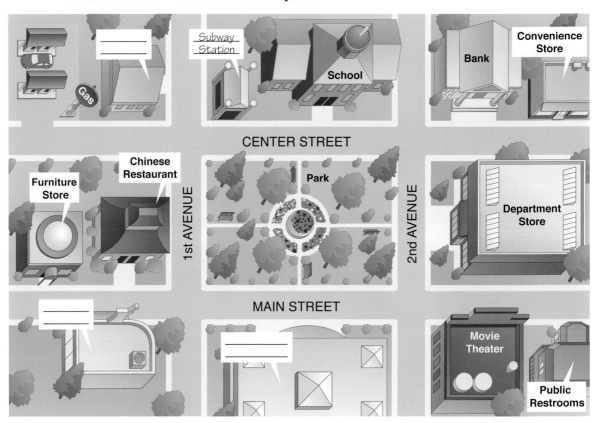

2 Ask about your partner's neighborhood. Choose (✓) *Yes* or *No*. Write extra information on the line.

> **Is there a bank in your neighborhood?**

> Yes, there is. It's next to the subway station.

	Yes	No	Extra information
1. Is there a bank in your neighborhood?	☐	☐	_____
2. Is there a department store?	☐	☐	_____
3. Is there a park?	☐	☐	_____
4. Is there a gas station?	☐	☐	_____
5. Is there a drugstore?	☐	☐	_____

UNITS 10–12 *What did they do?*
Student A

1 **PAIR WORK. Ask and answer questions to complete the information.**

A What did <u>Albert</u> do last weekend?

B <u>He went shopping</u>. What did he do yesterday?

A <u>He went to the bank</u>. What did he do last night?

B <u>He went to a party</u>.

	Last Weekend	Yesterday	Last Night
Albert	He went shopping.	*First Bank*	He went to a party.
Jessica			
Maria and Tony			

2 **Ask about your partner. Complete the sentences.**

1. My partner _____ last weekend.
2. He/She _____ yesterday.
3. He/She _____ last night.
4. He/She _____ this morning.

> **What did you do ... ?**

UNITS 1–3 *What's his phone number?*
Student B

1 **PAIR WORK. Ask and answer questions to complete the information.**

A What's <u>Mike's</u> phone number?

B His phone number is <u>749-6345</u>. What's <u>his</u> email address?

A <u>His</u> email address is <u>mike@net.com</u>.

1. **Name:** Mike Johnson
   Phone: 749-6345
   Email: <u>mike@net.com</u>
   Job: _____
   Hobby: photography

2. **Name:** Julia Rivera
   Phone: 527-3411
   Email: _____
   Job: _____
   Hobby: biking

3. **Name:** Amy Hooper
   Phone: 355-0830
   Email: _____
   Job: student
   Hobby: _____

4. **Name:** Richard Wong
   Phone: _____
   Email: rich23@me.net
   Job: _____
   Hobby: tennis

2 **Ask about your partner. Complete the sentences.**

1. My partner's name is _____.
2. His/Her phone number is _____.
3. His/Her email address is _____.
4. His/Her mother's name is _____.
5. His/Her father's name is _____.
6. His/Her hobby is _____.

> **What's your ... ?**

> **What's your mother's ... ?**

> **What's your father's ... ?**

UNITS 4–6 *What can they do well?*
Student B

1 **PAIR WORK. Ask and answer questions to complete the chart.**

A What can <u>Alan</u> do very well?
B He can <u>speak Chinese</u> very well. What can he do well?
A He can <u>play the piano</u> well. What *can't* he do?
B He can't <u>do yoga</u> at all.

	Very well	Well	Not at all
Alan	speak Chinese	play the piano	do yoga
Meg		play the guitar	
Kazu and Hiro	play soccer		swim
Jen		cook	

2 **Ask and answer questions to complete the sentences.**

1. My partner can _____ well.
2. My partner can _____ very well.
3. My partner can't _____ at all.
4. My partner's friends can _____ well.
5. My partner's friends can't _____ at all.

> **What can you do … ?**

> **What can your friends do … ?**

UNITS 7–9 *Where's the subway station?*
Student B

1 **PAIR WORK.** Ask and answer questions to complete the map. Ask about the places in the box.

> department store   convenience store   furniture store   public restrooms

A Where's the <u>subway station</u>?

B It's on <u>Center Street</u>. It's <u>across from the park</u>.

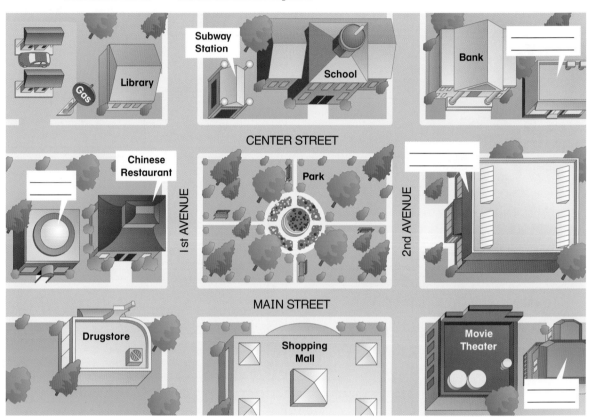

2 Ask about your partner's neighborhood. Choose (✓) *Yes* or *No*. Write extra information on the line.

> **Is there a bank in your neighborhood?**
>
> **Yes, there is. It's next to the subway station.**

	Yes	No	Extra information
1. Is there a bank in your neighborhood?	☐	☐	_____
2. Is there a department store?	☐	☐	_____
3. Is there a park?	☐	☐	_____
4. Is there a gas station?	☐	☐	_____
5. Is there a drugstore?	☐	☐	_____

UNITS 10–12 *What did they do?*
Student B

1 **PAIR WORK. Ask and answer questions to complete the information.**

A What did <u>Albert</u> do last weekend?
B <u>He went shopping</u>. What did he do yesterday?
A <u>He went to the bank</u>. What did he do last night?
B <u>He went to a party</u>.

	Last Weekend	Yesterday	Last Night
Albert		He went to the bank.	
Jessica			
Maria and Tony			

2 **Ask about your partner. Complete the sentences.**

1. My partner _____ last weekend.
2. He/She _____ yesterday.
3. He/She _____ last night.
4. He/She _____ this morning.

> **What did you do … ?**

UNITS 1–3

1 Read this information about Selena Gomez. Then complete the article about her.

Celebrity Profile

1.	What's her name?	Selena Gomez
2.	What's her nickname?	Sel
3.	What's her job?	singer and actor
4.	Where's she from?	Texas, USA
5.	When's her birthday?	July 22nd
6.	What's her hobby?	surfing
7.	What's her favorite food?	pizza
8.	Who's her favorite singer?	Kehlani

Selena Gomez is from ___Texas___. Her nickname is _____. She's a _____ and an actor.

Her _____ is July 22nd. Her _____ is surfing. Her _____ _____ is pizza. Her _____ is Kehlani.

2 **PAIR WORK.** Ask your partner questions like the ones above. Then write about your partner.

My partner's name is Toshinori Miura. His nickname is Tommy. He's from Yokohama, Japan. His favorite food is …

UNITS 4–6

1 **Look at the photos of Clark's friends. Complete the text.**

I have amazing friends! These are photos of my friends.

Ellen _____ play the guitar. She only plays at home. Mark and Jennifer _____ tennis very well. They _____ _____ on the weekend. This is David. He _____ rock music and hip-hop, but he can't _____ at all! Keith and Matt _____ video games online every day. And this is Aiko. She _____ _____ with her friends every Saturday.

Ellen

David

Mark and Jennifer

Keith and Matt

Aiko

2 **What can your friends do well? What do they do for fun? Complete the chart. Then write about your friends.**

	Name	He/she can ...	He/she likes ...
1.			
2.			
3.			
4.			
5.			

My friend Diego likes classical music. He can cook, play the piano, and do yoga. My friend Min-sook likes ...

UNITS 7–9

1 Complete the text message. Use the words in the box. Two words are not used.

| fun | boots | Fifth Street | dancing | singing |

From: Mark
To: Dave

At the karaoke!
today, 12:40 PM

Hey Dave!
What are you doing? I'm at the new karaoke place on _____ . Do you know it? It's next to the Chinese restaurant. It's great! I'm with Maria and Josh. We're singing a lot, but not very well. Look at this picture. Do you like my new shirt?
I'm _____ "Love Me Tender" by Elvis.
It's _____ .
See you soon!

Mark

2 Where are you now? What are you doing? Answer the questions.
Then write a text message like the one above.

1. Where are you?   I'm at _____.
2. Where is that place?   It's on _____, across from/next to _____.
3. What's in that place?   There's an _____ and some _____.
4. What are you doing?   I'm _____.
5. What are you not doing? I'm not _____.
6. What are you wearing?   I'm wearing _____.
7. Are you having fun?   _____.

Right now, I'm at a coffee shop. It's on Main Street, next to the subway station. There's a sofa and some comfortable chairs in it. I'm drinking coffee and doing my homework. Well, actually, I'm not doing homework! I'm talking to my friends! I'm wearing a …

UNITS 10–12

1 **Complete the sentences with the words in the box.**

crowded	stay	went	bored	interesting	visited

Here are some photos from my summer vacation. I _____ to Rio de Janeiro. I _____ the city with my brother and sister. Rio was really _____ . We didn't _____ at the hotel at all! There was so much to do. We were never _____ . Our hotel was next to Ipanema beach. Although there were a lot of people, the beach wasn't _____ . It was so big! We saw people playing beach volleyball.

We saw a lot of different places. We went to the top of the Sugar Loaf Mountain. We visited the Museum of Modern Art.

It was a great vacation. I had a lot of fun, and I want to go back!

Ipanema Beach

Sugar Loaf Mountain

Museum of Modern Art, Rio

2 **Complete the chart with information about your last vacation. Then write about it.**

	My Last Vacation
When?	
Where?	
What activities?	

Last year, I went to Greece. It was great! I ate some interesting food. I also …

UNIT 1

LISTENING .... p. 8

1. **Mark** Hi, I'm Mark. Welcome to London!
   Sara Nice to meet you. I'm Sara.
   M Are you from the US, Sara?
   S No, I'm not. I'm from Canada.

2. **Maria** Hi, John, how are you?
   John Good, thanks. How about you, Maria?
   M Great! So, are you a student here?
   J Yes, I am.

3. **A** Look! It's Tom Cruise! Hey, Tom!
   B Tom Cruise? He's not Tom Cruise.
   A What?
   B He's not Tom Cruise. He's Brad Pitt!
   A Oh!... Brad! Hey, Brad!

4. **Ted** Hi, I'm Ted Tucker.
   Paula Hi, Ted. I'm Paula Rosario. Nice to meet you.
   T Nice to meet you, too. Are you a businesswoman?
   P No, I'm not. I'm an engineer.

LISTENING PLUS .... p. 8

Paula So, Ted, are you from the US?
Ted Yes, I am. How about you, Paula?
P I'm not from the US.
T Where are you from?
P I'm from Vancouver.
T Vancouver?
P Yes, it's in Canada. Are you from New York?
T No, I'm not from New York.
P Where in the US are you from?
T I'm from New Jersey.

UNIT 2

LISTENING .... p. 14

1. **Loyd** Do you want to go swimming on Saturday, Fiona?
   Fiona I'd love to, Loyd. My favorite hobby is swimming. What time on Saturday?
   L I'm not sure. What's your phone number? I'll call you.
   F It's 3-2-7 – 9-2-0-3.
   L I'm sorry. Can you repeat that?
   F Sure. It's 3-2-7 – 9-2-0-3.
   L OK. 3-2-7...92...03. Got it.

2. **Michael** What great photos! You are a really great photographer!
   Tricia Thank you, Michael. I love photography. What's your email address? I'll send you those photos.
   M It's mike@school.edu.
   T OK. m-i-k-e at school dot edu. Is Mike your nickname?
   M Yes, it is.

3. **April** ...and I think you'll like the cycling club, Kyoko.
   Kyoko Thank you, April. I love cycling.
   A So, what's your address?
   K It's 23 Park Street.
   A And what's your phone number?
   K My phone number? It's 524-9056.
   A OK. 524...90..96.
   K No, it's 524-9056.

4. **Meyer** Hi, Dana, How are you?
   Dana Great, Meyer. How about you?
   M Good, thanks. Hey, when's your birthday?
   D It's October 7th.
   M October 11th?
   D No, October 7th.
   M Oh, OK. Hey, that's today! Happy Birthday!
   D Thanks.
   M What are you going to do for your birthday?
   D Well, I love tennis, so I'm going to buy a new tennis racket.
   M Wow. Nice!

LISTENING PLUS .... p. 14

Loyd Can I have your home phone number, too, Fiona?
Fiona My home phone number?
L Yes, your home phone number.
F It's 577-394-2769.
L 577-394-2769. OK. And what's your address?
F It's 30 West Street.
L 20 West Street?
F No, not 20 West Street. It's 30 West Street.
L Oh, OK. 30 West Street. Got it. Now, when is your birthday?
F It's September 8th.
L September 8th. And what's your driver's license number?
F It's 109-142-8375.
L Can you repeat that, please?
F Sure. 109...142...8375.
L Great. Thank you!

UNIT 3

LISTENING . . . . p. 20

1. **Friend** These are nice photos! Who's this?
   May It's my friend, Linda.
   F Is she from Brazil?
   M No, she just loves yellow.

2. **A** These are cute dogs!
   B Thanks. This is Teddy and this is Toby.
   A Are these your dogs?
   B The white dog, Teddy, is mine. Toby is Tina's dog.
   A Who's Tina?
   B She's a friend from school.

3. **B** And this is my first computer.
   A Wow, it's really old. Is it a laptop?
   B Well, yes, but it's really heavy.
   A Yeah, it looks heavy!

4. **A** Is this your car?
   B No, it isn't. It's my father's car. He loves old cars.
   A Me, too. That's a really nice color. What kind of car is it?
   B I have no idea.

LISTENING PLUS . . . . p. 20

1. **Friend** So, is Linda a friend from school?
   May No, she's a friend from work.
   F How old is she?
   M Let me see… She's thirty-two, I think.

2. **A** How old is Toby?
   B I don't know.
   A You don't know how old your friend is?
   B You mean Tina. Tina's my friend from school, not Toby. Toby is her dog!
   A Oh, sorry.
   B Tina is about twenty-five, I'd say.

3. **A** So, how old is the computer?
   B It's about… let me see. Fifteen years old.
   A That's really old for a computer. Do you use it?
   B No, not really.

4. **A** Wow, what a great car. How old is it?
   B Let me think… maybe thirty-five years old? I'm not sure.
   A Hmm… And where does your father live?
   B He lives here.
   A Great! I want to drive that car!

UNIT 4

LISTENING . . . . p. 28

1. **Sofia** Hey, Jim, do you like hip-hop?
   Jim Hip-hop? No, I think hip-hop is terrible, Sofia.
   S Terrible? Why?
   J Well, I think the music is annoying.
   S How about pop music? Do you like pop music?
   J No, I don't like pop music. I think it's boring.
   S So, you don't like pop music or hip-hop. How about classical music?
   J Yes, I like classical music. I think classical music is very pleasant.

2. **Ken** How about you, Mary? Do you like music?
   Mary I love music, Ken.
   K Do you like jazz?
   M Um… well, actually, I don't. I think jazz is annoying.
   K Annoying? Really? Do you like Latin music?
   M Yes, I do. I like Enrique Iglesias.

3. **Cathy** What about dance music? Who likes dance music? Frank?
   Frank Not me, Cathy. Ugh! Dance music? No way!
   C Really? How about rock music? Do you like rock music, Frank?
   F I do, actually. I think rock music is good.

4. **Johnny** Do you like rock music, Karen?
   Karen Um… It's not bad.
   J Not bad?
   K Well, actually, Johnny… I don't like it.
   J Do you like dance music?
   K Yes, I do. I think dance music is catchy.

LISTENING PLUS . . . . **p. 28**

1. **Sophia** So, Jim… you like classical music. Who's your favorite musician?

   Jim Well, I really like Beethoven. You know, I like classical music, but jazz is my favorite kind of music.

   S Jazz?

   J Yes, jazz. I think classical music is pleasant, but jazz is my favorite.

2. **Ken** How about you, Mary? You like Latin music. Is it your favorite kind of music?

   Mary Yes, it is. I love Latin music, especially Enrique Iglesias! He's amazing!

3. **Cathy** And is rock music your favorite kind of music, Frank?

   Frank Um… I like rock music, but it's not my favorite.

   C Really? So, what is your favorite kind of music, Frank?

   F Classical music. I love Mozart.

4. **Johnny** Do you like Mozart, Karen?

   Karen Mozart? He's… OK.

   J You like dance music, right?

   K Yes, I do, but it's not my favorite kind of music.

   J It isn't? What is your favorite kind of music, Karen?

   K Hip-hop. Hip-hop is amazing!

LISTENING . . . . **p. 34**

1. **Adam** Hi, Mara.

   Mara Hi, Adam. Wow…Is that a new phone?

   A Yes, it is. I really like it.

   M Do you play games on it?

   A Yes, I do, and I surf the web.

   M Do you upload videos?

   A No, I don't. How about you? Do you play games on your phone?

   M No, I don't…I send text messages.

2. **Jackie** Hey, Peter.

   Peter Hi, Jackie.

   J Hey! Let's go shopping on the weekend!

   P Shopping? I don't like to go shopping. I only shop online!

   J Oh… Well, what do you do for fun, Peter?

   P I have coffee with friends.

   J Really? That sounds… a little boring.

   P OK… Well, do you like bowling?

   J No, not really.

   P Oh, OK.

   J Sorry, Peter.

LISTENING PLUS . . . . **p. 34**

1. **Jackie** Hi, Adam.

   Adam Oh, hey, Jackie.

   J Are you free on Friday?

   A Yes, I am.

   J Do you want to do yoga together?

   A Um, I don't do yoga.

   J Oh, I do yoga every Friday. Hmm… Are you free on Sunday?

   A No, I'm not. I play tennis with my friends every Sunday. How about Saturday?

   J I'm free on Saturday. Peter doesn't want to go shopping with me.

   A I go shopping on Saturdays. Let's go shopping together!

   J OK, great!

UNIT 6

LISTENING .... p. 40

1. **Lucas** Let's go to a restaurant, Yuko!
   Yuko Well, Lucas, uh, let's just stay home and cook.
   L Can you cook?
   Y Sure! I can cook really well. I love to cook at home.

2. **Phoebe** Wow, Jake! You can sing!
   Jake Oh, well, Phoebe. I don't know...
   P No, really. You can sing very well!
   J Thanks.

3. **Sean** Hey, Laura, let's do something fun.
   Laura Sure, like what, Sean?
   S I don't know. I can play the guitar. Can you sing?
   L No, not really.

4. **Andy** Hey, Ben, can you play video games?
   Ben Me? No, I can't play video games at all. I don't like video games.
   A So let's do something else. Can you play tennis?
   B Tennis? I love tennis!
   A Me, too. Let's play! Let's go to my tennis club.

LISTENING PLUS .... p. 40

1. **Andy** Wow, Ben. You can play tennis really well.
   Ben Thanks, Andy. You can play well, too.
   A Well, not really...
   B Yes, you can!
   A Well, I guess I'm OK. Do you play often?
   B Yes, I do. I play every day. I play at school with friends. I sometimes play with my parents.
   A With your parents? How old are your parents?
   B My mother is 48 and my father is 50.
   A Wow. My parents can't play tennis. They don't play any sports.

UNIT 7

LISTENING .... p. 48

1. **Officer** OK, Mrs. Farkas. Can you see those men?
   Mrs. Farkas Yes, I can see them, officer.
   O Good. Now, which one is the bank robber?
   F Let me see... Ah, yes. It's that one!
   O Which one?
   F That man, right there. He's wearing jeans, and a green sweater.
   O Jeans, and a green sweater.. OK. Got it.
   F And he's wearing white sneakers, too.

2. **Jim** Hello?
   Olivia Hey, Jim! It's Olivia.
   J Hi, Olivia.
   O I'm at the train station. Where are you?
   J I'm at the train station, too. I'm wearing a blue shirt. I'm also wearing a gray suit. Can you see me?
   O A blue shirt and a gray suit. So you are in business clothes.... Hmm... Wait! Are you reading a book?
   J No. I'm drinking coffee.
   O Oh! There you are. I see you now!

3. **Isabelle** Hello?
   Mike Hello, Isabelle? It's Mike. Are you ready for our date?
   I Uh-huh. I'm here at the cafe. Where are you?
   M I'm here, too. But I can't see you. What are you doing?
   I I'm talking on the phone!
   M Very funny! OK, what are you wearing?
   I I'm wearing a black skirt and a white shirt. Oh, and I'm wearing black boots.
   M I think I see you. Are you wearing a white flower in your hair?
   I Yes, I am.

4. **A** Hey, look! Is that our boss, Mr. Gordon?
   B I don't know. I can't see him. Where is he?
   A He's on the dance floor!
   B I still can't see him. Is he wearing jeans?
   A No. He's wearing a suit and black shoes.
   B What's he doing? Is he just standing there?
   A No... he's dancing!
   B Really? Oh, yes, I see him now. Oh, man!
   A He can't dance at all!

LISTENING PLUS . . . . p. 48

Mike	Hello?
Isabelle	Hello, Mike? It's Isabelle.
M	Hi, Isabelle! How are you?
I	I'm great, thanks. How are you?
M	I'm OK. Hey, thanks for a wonderful afternoon yesterday. I had a great time on our date.
I	No, thank you. It was fun!
M	Are you doing anything now?
I	I'm watching TV. Hey, do you want to come over to my place and watch a movie?
M	That sounds great, but I'm cooking dinner.
I	Oh, you're cooking? So, you're busy...
M	Do you want to come over for dinner?
I	Sure! That sounds nice.

UNIT 8

LISTENING . . . . p. 54

1. A Where's my guitar?
   B I think it's in the living room.
   A I'm sorry. Where?
   B In the living room, under a sofa.
   A A sofa?
   B Yes, the red sofa.

2. A Where are my headphones?
   B There are headphones in the living room, behind the laptop.
   A Those aren't my headphones. Those are yours.
   B Oh, here they are. They're on the table in the kitchen.

3. Leo Hey John, can I check my e-mail?
   John Sorry, my computer is really old. Actually, I think it's broken.
   L Oh, OK. Are there any computers at school?
   J No, there aren't. You can use my cell phone.
   L Thanks, John.

4. A Where's my cell phone?
   B Hmm... There's a cell phone on the desk.
   A Where?
   B On the desk. The desk in the bedroom.
   A But that isn't my phone. Oh, here it is. It's in my bag. Never mind!

LISTENING PLUS . . . . p. 54

1. A Oh, here's my guitar. Hey, did you see my wallet?
   B Your wallet?
   A Yes, I'm looking for my wallet. You know, the brand new one.
   B I think it's in the kitchen, on the table.

2. A OK, I have my headphones. Is my book in the kitchen, too?
   B Well, there's a cookbook.
   A No, my English book.
   B Your English book is on the sofa in the living room.
   A Great. Thanks!

3. John I'm going to work now.
   Leo OK. See you later.
   J Hmm... Where are my glasses?
   L Your glasses? There's a pair of glasses in the bathroom.

4. A Well, I found my phone... but where's my sweater?
   B Your sweater?
   A Yes, my blue sweater.
   B There's a sweater in the kitchen, on a chair.

UNIT 9

LISTENING . . . . p. 60

1. A Excuse me. Where's the park?
   B There's one between the drugstore and the public restrooms.
   A Oh, I know that drugstore. It's on Smith Street.
   B That's right. It's very near here. You just go straight and cross Second Street.
   A Got it. Thanks!
   B No problem.

2. A Excuse me. Where's the subway station?
   B It's on First Street.
   A On First Street?
   B Yes, on First Street, next to the furniture store.
   A Thank you, but where's First Street?
   B Oh, it's very close. Just go straight on Smith Street.
   A Thank you!

3. **A** Hi, can you help me? Is there a gas station near here?

   B Let me think... Yes, there's a gas station on Second Street.

   A On Second Street?

   B Yeah. Go straight on Smith Street and turn right at the corner. The gas station is next to the convenience store.

   A Great. But, one question... Where's Smith Street?

   B Smith Street? It's right here! This is Smith Street.

   A Oh! Now I understand! Thanks so much!

4. **A** Hi. Is there a post office near here?

   B I don't know... Oh yes, there is. It's across from the police station.

   A The police station. That's on Second Street, right?

   B Actually, no. It's on First Street. You go straight on Smith Street and cross Second Street. Then turn right on First Street.

   A Straight on Smith, cross Second, right on First. OK.

   B And the post office is across from the police station.

   A Great. Thanks for your help!

LISTENING PLUS . . . . p. 60

A Excuse me. Are there any public restrooms near here?

B Hmm... Well, there are restrooms in the furniture store.

A Where's the furniture store?

B It's on First Street, but it's not near here.

A OK... well... thanks. How about the convenience store? Are there restrooms in the convenience store?

B No, there aren't. Oh, I know! There are public restrooms next to the park.

A Where's the park?

B Just go straight on Smith Street and cross Second Street. The park is on Smith Street.

A OK. Straight on Smith and cross Second.

B That's right.

A And the public restrooms are next to the park?

B Yes. They're on the corner of Smith Street and First Street.

A OK. Thanks a lot!

UNIT 10

LISTENING . . . . p. 68

1. **A** I'm thirsty. Hey, look at this fruit drink.

   B Let's make it!

   A OK. What do we need?

   B First, we need milk.

   A OK, we have some milk.

   B And we need juice. Do we have any juice?

   A Hmm... No, we don't. But we can get some.

   B OK, and we need a large banana and three apples.

   A Well, we have a large banana, but we only have two apples.

2. **A** Hey, are you hungry? Look at this Monster Sandwich!

   B Let's make it! Do we have any bread?

   A Yeah, we have some bread.

   B Great! What about chicken? Do we have any chicken?

   A Yes, there's some chicken in the refrigerator.

   B All right! And apples. Oh, and some lettuce. Do we have apples and lettuce?

   A Sorry. We have three apples, but there isn't any lettuce.

3. **A** What do you want to make for dinner?

   B How about this, "Auntie's Indian Dinner"?

   A Oh, that looks great. But we don't have any potatoes.

   B Oh... But we have some chicken and some fish, right?

   A Hmm... Actually, no. There isn't any chicken. And we don't have any fish. But there is some rice.

   B Oh, well. Let's just order a pizza.

4. **A** Wow, look at this dessert! It looks great!

   B Yeah—but is it good for you?

   A No, but I don't care. Let's make it.

   B All right. We need some ice cream and some cookies.

   A Let me look. We have some ice cream, but there aren't any cookies.

   B What about bananas and milk?

   A We don't have any bananas. And there isn't any milk.

   B OK, so let's go buy some cookies, bananas, and milk.

LISTENING PLUS................... p. 68

1. **A** I can't wait to make this dessert! It looks really good.
   B Oh, no! The supermarket is closed!
   A It's closed? But what can we make for dinner now?
   B Let's order a large pizza!
   A I don't want to order pizza again. What about this recipe for an Indian dinner?
   B Um, I don't really like Indian food.
   A You don't like Indian food?
   B No, I don't.
   A Well, what do you want to make?
   B How about this Monster Sandwich?
   A What do we need?
   B We need some bread, some lettuce, some chicken, and some apples.
   A We don't have any apples.
   B Yes, we do. They're in the refrigerator.
   A Let's make the Monster Sandwich then.
   B OK!

UNIT 11

LISTENING .... p. 74

1. **Mark** Hey, Suzie. Were you at work yesterday?
   Suzie No, Mark I wasn't. I was at the doctor's office. I wasn't at work yesterday or on Monday.
   M Really? Were you sick?
   S Yeah, but I'm OK now.
   M I'm glad you're feeling better.

2. **Rich** Hi, Andy! How are you?
   Andy I'm a little tired, Rich. I was at work pretty late yesterday.
   R And you were at school today?
   A Yes. I'm really busy at school and at work.
   R What are you studying this semester?
   A Economics. Right now, I'm writing a paper.
   R Were you at the library on the weekend?
   A No, I wasn't. Actually, I was at work.
   R You *are* busy!

3. **George** Tina! You look happy!
   Tina Yeah, George, yesterday was great!
   G Really? Why?
   T Well, I wasn't at work. I was at the mall all day. It was great.
   G Were you at work on Thursday?
   T Yes, I was. It was awful. I was so busy.

4. **Patty** Mark, were you at the gym last night?
   Mark No, Patty, I was there this morning. I was really bored, so I went to the library.
   P The library?
   M Yes, it was fun. I was there with some friends.

LISTENING PLUS................... p. 74

1. **Mark** How was your weekend, Suzie? Were you sick on Saturday and Sunday, too?
   Suzie I was sick on Sunday, but Saturday was great. I was at the gym all day.
   M You were at the gym all day? I hate the gym!
   S Really? I love it. I go there with some friends every Saturday.

2. **Andy** Yeah, I have been really busy. And yesterday was my birthday!
   Rich Your birthday? Andy, I didn't know that! Happy birthday!
   A Thanks!
   R How was your birthday? Were you at work?
   A Yeah, I was.
   R Oh, that's awful.

3. **George** I was at the mall on Saturday. Were you there, too, Tina?
   Tina No, I wasn't. I was at the supermarket. But I was at the mall on Sunday!
   G Really? Again?
   T Yeah... I guess I go to the mall a lot.

4. **Patty** Were you at the gym yesterday morning, too, Mark?
   Mark No, I wasn't. I was at the park.
   P At the park?
   M Yes. The weather was great. My friends were there. One of them has a dog! It was a lot of fun.

UNIT 12

LISTENING .... p. 80

1. **Thomas**   Hi, Kate. Did you stay home this weekend?

     Kate   No, I didn't. I took a trip.

     T   Really? Where did you go?

     K   I went to New York City. It was great!

     T   Oh, who did you go with?

     K   I went with my brother.

2. **Henry**   Hi, Dave. What did you do this weekend?

     Dave   On Saturday I went to work. I'm really busy these days, Henry.

     H   That's too bad. Did you have any fun?

     D   Yes, I did. On Sunday afternoon I went to a movie with Linda.

     H   Oh, how was the movie?

     D   Actually, it was not very interesting. But I think Linda liked it.

3. **Cynthia**   Good weekend, Angela?

     Angela   Oh, It wasn't bad, Cynthia.

     C   What did you do? Did you go somewhere?

     A   No, not really. I mean, on Saturday I went to the gym, the library, and the supermarket.

     C   That doesn't sound fun!

     A   Well, it was! I met someone at the supermarket!

4. **Ashton**   Good morning, Bob! Did you have a good weekend?

     Bob   Um, not really, Ashton. Well, I went out for dinner with Mary, the girl I like. We ate pizza.

     A   That's great!

     B   Not really. The restaurant was very noisy. Mary talked on her cell phone all night. And the pizza was cold.

LISTENING PLUS .... p. 80

1. **Thomas**   What did you do last night, Kate?

     Kate   Last night? Nothing interesting. I just stayed home.

     T   You stayed home?

     K   Yes. I was tired.

2. **Henry**   What did you do on Sunday night, Dave?

     Dave   On Sunday night? I don't remember... Oh, yes. Linda and I hung out with some friends.

     H   Did you go to a party?

     D   No, we just hung out with friends at Linda's house.

3. **Cynthia**   You met someone at the supermarket? Wow, Angela! Did you hang out with him on Sunday?

     Angela   Well, no. I went to the library on Sunday.

     C   The library?

     A   Yeah, I had a lot of homework. So, on Sunday I went to the library and I did my homework. But maybe next weekend!

4. **Ashton**   Oh. That's too bad, Bob. Well, did you do anything else on the weekend?

     Bob   Um, I cleaned my room... I just stayed home, really.

     A   Did you do your homework?

     B   My homework?

     A   Yes, the English homework.

     B   Oh... I forgot!

GRAMMAR

UNIT 1
The verb *be*: statements and questions with contractions

We use the simple present of *be* to talk about things like names, nationalities, and jobs.

- *His name **is** Bill.*
- *I **am** from Costa Rica.*
- *My teacher **is** from the United States.*
- *They **are** students here.*

We often contract, or shorten, the verb *be*.

- *He**'s** a businessman.*
- *We**'re** students.*
- *He **isn't** a teacher.*
- *We **aren't** writers.*

Affirmative statements		
I	am 'm	
You We They	are 're	from Rio.
He She It	is 's	

Negative statements		
I	am not 'm not	
You We They	are not aren't 're not	from New York
He She It	is not isn't 's not	

We often contract negative short answers.

- *No, I**'m** not.*
- *No, they **aren't**.*

We only use full forms in affirmative short answers.

- *Yes, I am. (Yes, I'm.)*
- *Yes, he is. (Yes, he's.)*

Yes/No questions		
Are	you we they	from Rio?
Is	he she	

Short answers	
Yes, I **am**.	No, I**'m not**.
Yes, we **are**.	No, we **aren't**./No, we**'re not**.
Yes, they **are**.	No, they **aren't**./No, they**'re not**.
Yes, he **is**.	No, he **isn't**./No, he**'s not**.
Yes, she **is**.	No, she **isn't**./No, she**'s not**.
Yes, it **is**.	No, it **isn't**./No, it**'s not**.

NOW PRACTICE

1 Complete the statements. Use *am*, *is*, or *are*.

1. Mr. Li _____is_____ a businessman from South Korea.
2. Bill and John _____ students here.
3. Ms. Garcia _____ a chef.
4. Mr. Jones and Mr. Taylor _____ teachers here.
5. I _____ a good student.

UNIT 2
The verb *be*: *wh-* questions

We use *wh-* questions to ask about things, people, places, times, and dates.

Use *what* to ask about things.
- **What** *is her phone number?*
- **What** *is his name?*

Use *who* to ask about people.
- **Who** *is your favorite actor?*
- **Who** *is your teacher?*

Use *where* to ask about places.
- **Where** *are you from?*
- **Where** *is Vancouver?*

Use *when* to ask about times, dates, etc.
- **When** *is your birthday?*
- **When** *is our chemistry class?*

We can contract, or shorten, some question words with is.
- **What's** *her name? (What's = What is)*
- **Who's** *he? (Who's = Who is)*
- **Where's** *he from? (Where's = Where is)*
- **When's** *your English class?(When's = When is)*

Wh- questions							
Where	is 's	he she it	from?	Where	**are**	you we they	from?
Where	is 's	his her its	book?	Where	**are**	your our their	books?

NOW PRACTICE

1 Complete the conversations. Use *what, who, where,* or *when*.

1. A <u> What </u> is your phone number?
   B It's 555-4938.

2. A _____ is Curitiba?
   B It's in Brazil.

3. A _____ is your favorite food?
   B My favorite food is pizza.

4. A _____ is Oda Yuji?
   B He's a Japanese actor.

5. A _____ is your birthday?
   B It's in December.

6. A _____ are your favorite singers?
   B Renato Russo and Marisa Monte.

2 Complete the questions. Use contractions where possible.

1. <u> What's </u> your teacher's name?
2. _____ New York?
3. _____ Tokyo and Osaka?
4. _____ their favorite actors?
5. _____ his nickname?
6. _____ her birthday?

UNIT 3
Demonstrative pronouns: *this, that, these,* and *those*

We use *this* (singular) and *these* (plural) for people and things that are near us.

- **This** *is my camera.*

- **These** *are my photos.*

We use *that* (singular) and *those* (plural) for people and things that are not near us.

- **That** *is my camera.*

- **Those** *are my photos.*

Yes/No questions	Short answers	
Is **this** your wallet?	Yes, **it** is.	No, **it** isn't.
Is **that** your teacher?	Yes, **it** is.	No, **it** isn't.
Are **these** your books?	Yes, **they** are.	No, **they** aren't.
Are **those** your books?	Yes, **they** are.	No, **they** aren't.

NOW PRACTICE

1 Complete the questions. Use *is this* or *are these*.

1. ___Are___ ___these___ your books?
2. _____ _____ your phone number?
3. _____ _____ your photos?
4. _____ _____ your friends?
5. _____ _____ your favorite food?

2 Complete the conversations. Use *it is, it isn't, they are, they aren't*.

1. **A** Is that your brother?
   B Yes, ___it is___.

2. **A** Is that our server?
   B No, _____.

3. **A** Are these your photos?
   B Yes, _____.

4. **A** Is this your wallet?
   B Yes, _____.

5. **A** Is this her camera?
   B No, _____.

6. **A** Are those your friends?
   B Yes, _____.

UNIT 4

The simple present with *like*

We use *like* or *likes* (like + -s) in affirmative statements.

Affirmative statements					
I You We They	**like**	jazz.	He She It	**likes**	jazz.

We use *do not like* or *does not like* in negative statements.

Negative statements					
I You We They	**do not like**	hip-hop.	He She It	**does not like**	hip-hop.

We often contract, or shorten, *do not* and *does not*.

- I **don't** like jazz. (don't = do not)
- She **doesn't** like hip-hop. (doesn't = does not)

We use *do* or *does* in yes/no questions and short answers. We usually use contractions in negative short answers.

Yes/No questions			Short answers	
Do	you we they	**like** jazz?	Yes, I **do**. Yes, we **do**. Yes, they **do**.	No, I **do not**./No, I **don't**. No, we **do not**./No, we **don't**. No, they **do not**./No, they **don't**.
Does	he she it		Yes, he **does**. Yes, she **does**. Yes, it **does**.	No, he **does not**./No, he **doesn't**. No, she **does not**./No, she **doesn't**. No, it **does not**./No, it **doesn't**.

NOW PRACTICE

1 Complete the sentences with *like, likes, don't like,* or *doesn't like.*

1. My parents ___like___ jazz. They don't like rock music.
2. My friends _____ classical music. They like pop music.
3. I don't like electronica. I _____ hip-hop.
4. My brother likes dance music. He _____ jazz.

2 Complete the conversations. Use contractions where possible.

1. A _____Do_____ you like rock music?
   B Yes, I _____. I _____ it a lot.

2. A _____ your brother like jazz?
   B No, he _____. He _____ hip-hop.

3. A _____ your sister like dance music?
   B Yes, she _____. She _____ it a lot.

4. A _____ your friends like pop music?
   B No, they _____. They _____ jazz.

UNIT 5

The simple present: statements and *wh-* questions

We use the simple present for facts, habits, and routines.

- *My teacher* **speaks** *English.*
- *My friends and I* **like** *soccer.*

In questions, we use the helping verb *do* or *does* + a main verb. (*Do* can be a helping verb and a main verb.)

- *When* **do** *you* **play** *soccer?*
- *What* **do** *you* **do** *on Sunday?*

Notice the order of words in *wh-* questions:
wh- word + helping verb (*do* or *does*) + subject + main verb

Wh- questions			
Where	**do**	you we they	**go** shopping?
Where	**does**	he she	**go** shopping?

SPELLING RULES: third person singular

Some verbs end in *ch, sh, x,* or *ss.* Add *–es* to these verbs.

tea**ch**	+*es*	=	**teaches**
wa**sh**	+*es*	=	**washes**
fi**x**	+*es*	=	**fixes**
mi**ss**	+*es*	=	**misses**

Some verbs end in a consonant + *–y.* Change the *–y* to *–i* and add *–es.*

study	-*y* +*ies*	=	**studies**
try	-*y* +*ies*	=	**tries**

Three verbs have a special form:

do → **does**   go → **goes**   have → **has**

Add *–s* to other verbs.

play	+*s*	=	**plays**
read	+*s*	=	**reads**

NOW PRACTICE

1 Complete the sentences. Use the correct spelling of the verb in parentheses.

1. My teacher ___goes___ to school every day. (go)
2. My sister _____ TV every night. (watch)
3. My father _____ coffee every day. (have)
4. My brother _____ to rock music all the time. (listen)
5. My friend _____ his homework in class. (do)
6. My teacher _____ Mexican food. (like)

2 Complete the questions. Use *do* or *does* and a main verb in the box.

do	go	have	play

1. Where ___do___ you ___play___ tennis?
2. Where _____ you _____ after school?
3. When _____ your sister _____ yoga?
4. Where _____ your friends _____ coffee?

UNIT 6
Can and can't: statements and *yes/no* questions

We use the helping verb *can* + a main verb to talk about ability.
We use *cannot* or the contraction *can't* in negative statements.

Affirmative statements	Negative statements
I You He She **can draw.** It We They	I You He She **cannot sing/can't sing.** It We They

Notice the order of words in *yes/no* questions: *can* + subject + main verb.
We usually use the contraction *can't* in negative short answers.

Yes/No questions			Short answers	
	I		Yes, you **can.**	No, you **cannot.**/No, you **can't.**
	you		Yes, I **can.**	No, I **cannot.**/No, I **can't.**
	he		Yes, he **can.**	No, he **cannot.**/No, he **can't.**
Can	she	**help?**	Yes, she **can.**	No, she **cannot.**/No, she **can't.**
	it		Yes, it **can.**	No, it **cannot.**/No, it **can't.**
	we		Yes, we **can.**	No, we **cannot.**/No, we **can't.**
	they		Yes, they **can.**	No, they **cannot.**/No, they **can't.**

NOW PRACTICE

1 **Complete the sentences with *can* and *can't*. Use information about you.**

1. I _____ speak Spanish.
2. I _____ speak Japanese.
3. I _____ ride a bike.
4. My teacher _____ drive a car.
5. My friends and I _____ play tennis.

2 **Complete the conversations. Use contractions where possible.**

1. A ___Can___ your father ___play___ the guitar?
   B No, he ___can't___.

2. A _____ your sister _____ a bike?
   B Yes, she _____. She rides a bike to school every day.

3. A _____ your brother _____ French?
   B No, he _____. He only speaks Spanish.

4. A _____ you _____ Korean food?
   B No, I _____. I can only cook Mexican food.

UNIT 7

The present continuous: statements and questions

We can use the present continuous to talk about actions happening now.

- *I can't talk now. I'm studying.*
- *My sister isn't here now. She's playing tennis.*

For the present continuous, we use the helping verb *be* + –*ing* form of a main verb.
For negative statements, we use the helping verb *be* + *not* + –*ing* form of a main verb.

Affirmative statements			
I	am 'm	reading	a great book.
You We They	are 're	reading	a great book.
He She It	is 's	reading	a great book.

Negative statements			
I	am not 'm not	watching	TV.
You We They	are not aren't 're not	watching	TV.
He She It	is not isn't 's not	watching	TV.

In *yes/no* questions, we use the helping verb *be* + subject + -*ing* form of a main verb.

- **Are** you **using** this computer?
  Yes, I **am**.
- **Is** she **using** this computer?
  No, she **isn't**.

Notice the order of words in *wh-* questions:
Wh- word + the helping verb *be* + subject + -*ing* form of a main verb.

Wh- questions			
What	are	you we they	reading?
What	is	he she it	reading?

SPELLING RULES: -*ing* form		
wear	+*ing*	= wearing
do	+*ing*	= doing
study	+*ing*	= studying
read	+*ing*	= reading
drive	-*e* +*ing*	= driving
dance	-*e* +*ing*	= dancing
swim	double consonant + *ing*	= *swimming*
stop	double consonant + *ing*	= *stopping*

NOW PRACTICE

1 Complete the sentences. Use contractions if possible.

1. I <u>'m reading</u> a very good book. (read)
2. She _____ on the phone now. (talk)
3. We _____ English in school. (study)
4. My friends _____ a good movie. (watch)
5. He _____ his name. (write)
6. You _____ online. (shop)

2 Complete the questions with the present continuous form.

1. What <u>are</u> you <u>reading</u>? (read)
2. Where _____ they _____ tennis? (play)
3. What _____ you _____? (draw)
4. What _____ he _____? (cook)

UNIT 8

There is and *there are*

We use *there is/there are* to say that something exists (or doesn't exist).
We use *there is* with singular nouns. We use *there are* with plural nouns.

- **There is** *somebody at the door.*
- **There are** *15 students in my class.*

In affirmative statements, we often contract *there is*. We do not contract *there are*.

- **There's** *a lamp on the desk. (there's = there is)*

In negative statements, we often contract *there is not* and *there are not*.

- **There isn't** *a computer here. (there isn't = there is not)*
- **There aren't** *any computers here. (there aren't = there are not)*

Notice the order of words in *yes/no* questions: *be + there + subject*. We often contract negative short answers.

Yes/No questions				Short answers	
Is	**there**	a lamp	in the room?	Yes, **there is.**	No, **there isn't.**
Are	**there**	any lamps	in the room?	Yes, **there are.**	No, **there aren't.**

NOW PRACTICE

1 **Complete the sentences with *there's* or *there are*. Then write the negative sentences.**

1. _____There are_____ three windows in my classroom.
   _There aren't three windows in my classroom._____.

2. _____ a blue sofa in my apartment.
   _____.

3. _____ six chairs in my kitchen.
   _____.

4. _____ a computer in my bedroom.
   _____.

2 **Complete the conversations. Use contractions where possible.**

1. A _____Is there_____ a restaurant near your school?
   B Yes, _____there is_____.

2. A _____ curtains on the windows in your living room?
   B No, _____.

3. A _____ headphones in the drawer?
   B Yes, _____.

4. A _____ a chair in your bedroom?
   B No, _____.

UNIT 9
Prepositions of place

1. on

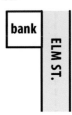

There's a bank on Elm Street.

2. across from

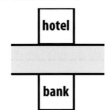

There's a bank across from the hotel.

3. next to

There's a hotel next to the bank.

4. on the corner of

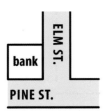

There's a bank on the corner of Pine and Elm.

5. between

There's a hotel between the bank and the park.

NOW PRACTICE

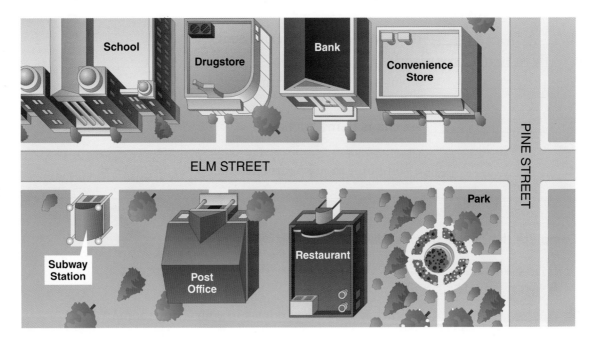

1 **Look at the map. Complete the sentences.**

1. There's a school _____*on*_____ Elm Street.
2. There's a subway station _____ the post office.
3. There's a drugstore _____ the school and the bank.
4. There's a convenience store _____ Elm and Pine.
5. There's a bank _____ the restaurant.

UNIT 10

Count and noncount nouns, *some* and *any*

Count nouns are things we can count. Count nouns can be singular or plural.

- 1 *apple*   2 *apples*
- 1 *potato*   2 *potatoes*
- 1 *banana*   2 *bananas*

We can use *a* or *an* with singular count nouns. We can use numbers with plural count nouns.

- I have **an** apple.
- I have **two** apples.

Noncount nouns are things we can't count. Noncount nouns have only one form.

- We need some **bread**.   We need some breads.
- We have some **milk**.   We have some milks.

We can't use *a*, *an*, or numbers with noncount nouns.

- We have some *rice*.   We have a rice.

We use a singular verb with a noncount noun.

- There **isn't** any bread on the table.
- There **is** some cake in the kitchen.

In affirmative statements, we can use *some* before noncount nouns and plural nouns.

- We need **some** milk.
- I have **some** apples.

In negative statements and questions, we can use *any* before noncount nouns and plural nouns.

- We don't need **any** milk.
- Do we have **any** apples?

NOW PRACTICE

1 Complete the sentences. Use *a, an, some,* or *any*.

1. There are ___some___ bananas in the kitchen.
2. There's _____ magazine on the table.
3. I need _____ computer.
4. Do you want _____ apple?
5. I don't have _____ sneakers.
6. I can drive _____ car.
7. We need _____ potatoes.
8. There aren't _____ bananas at the supermarket.
9. There isn't _____ milk on the table.
10. There are _____ new stores in town.

UNIT 11

The verb *be:* past statements and questions

The verb *be* has two forms in the past: *was* and *were*.

Affirmative statements					
I He She It	**was**	at home yesterday.	We You They	**were**	at home yesterday.

In negative statements, we often use contractions.

- She wasn't at school yesterday.
  (*wasn't = was not*)
- My friends weren't at school yesterday.
  (*weren't = were not*)

We use contractions *wasn't, weren't* in negative short answers but not in affirmative short answers.

- Was Isabella at school yesterday?
  No, she **wasn't**.
- Was Ken at school yesterday?
  Yes, he **was**.
- Were your parents at work yesterday?
  No, they **weren't**.
- Were your parents at home yesterday?
  Yes, they **were**.

We form *wh-* questions with a *wh-* word + *was* or *were* + subject.

Wh- questions							
Where	**was**	I he she it	yesterday?	Where	**were**	you we they	yesterday?

NOW PRACTICE

1 Complete the statements with *was, wasn't, were,* or *weren't.*
Use information about you.

1. I _____ at school yesterday.
2. My friends and I _____ at the library last night.
3. My teacher _____ in class yesterday.
4. My friends _____ at school last Sunday.

2 Complete the conversations with *was* or *were.*

1. **A** Where ___were___ you yesterday?
   B I ___was___ at the library.

2. **A** When _____ she at school yesterday?
   B In the morning.

3. **A** Where _____ your friends last night?
   B They _____ at home.

4. **A** Where _____ you last weekend?
   B I _____ at home.

UNIT 12

The simple past: statements and questions

We use the simple past for completed actions in the past.

- He **stayed** at home yesterday.
- We **went** to a party last night.

We add *–ed* for the simple past of most regular verbs. A few regular verbs have a special spelling.

Some verbs are irregular. There aren't any spelling rules for irregular verbs. Here are some examples.

Regular verbs			
Present			Past
play	+ed	=	played
talk	+ed	=	talked
listen	+ed	=	listened
like	+d	=	liked
hate	+d	=	hated
study	-y +ied	=	studied

Irregular verbs	
Present	Past
read	read
drive	drove
sing	sang
eat	ate
wear	wore
drink	drank
go	went

For negative statements and questions, we use the helping verb *did* + base form of the main verb.

Yes/No questions			Short answers					
Did	you he she it we they	**stay home?**	Yes,	I he she it we they	**did.**	No,	I he she it we they	**did not./didn't.**

NOW PRACTICE

1 **Complete the sentences with the regular verbs in parentheses.**

1. My brother and I __played__ tennis yesterday. (play)
2. I _____ your computer yesterday. (use)
3. She _____ to John last week. (not talk)
4. We _____ a great movie last week. (watch)
5. I _____ my room yesterday. (not clean)

2 **Answer the questions. Use information about you.**

1. Where did you go yesterday? _____.
2. What did you do last night? _____.
3. What did you eat this morning? _____.
4. What did you wear yesterday? _____.
5. What did you drink this morning? _____.

VOCABULARY

Unit 1

actor
artist
businessman
businesswoman
chef
engineer
model
programmer
server
singer
student
teacher
tour guide
web designer
writer

Good, thanks.
Hello.
Hi, I'm _____.
How about you?
How are you?
I'm from _____.
My name is _____.
Nice to meet you.
Nice to meet you, too.

Fine.
Great.
Not bad.
Not so good.
OK.
Pretty good.

Unit 2

address
birthday
cycling
email address
favorite food
favorite singer
hobby
home phone number
hometown
major
nickname
phone number
photography
swimming
tennis

biology
chemistry
English
history
math

at (@)
dash (-)
dot (.)
underscore (_)

0 – zero
1 – one
2 – two
3 – three
4 – four
5 – five
6 – six
7 – seven
8 – eight
9 – nine
10 – ten

January
February
March
April
May
June
July
August
September
October
November
December

Unit 3

an ATM card
a camera
a car
a cell phone
a computer
a credit card
a driver's license
glasses
headphones
keys
a laptop
money
a photo
a school ID card
textbooks
a wallet

brother
classmate
father
friend
neighbor
parents
sister

11 – eleven
12 – twelve
13 – thirteen
14 – fourteen
15 – fifteen
16 – sixteen
17 – seventeen
18 – eighteen
19 – nineteen

20 – twenty
30 – thirty
40 – forty
50 – fifty
60 – sixty
70 – seventy
80 – eighty
90 – ninety
100 – one hundred

black
blue
gray
green
red
white

Unit 4

classical music
dance music
electronica
hip-hop
jazz
Latin music
pop music
rock music

amazing
annoying
boring
catchy
great
fantastic
pleasant
terrible

Unit 5

do homework
do yoga
download apps
go bowling
go shopping
have coffee with friends
listen to music
play soccer
play tennis
play video games
read books
send text messages
shop online
upload videos
watch TV

at night
every week
on Sunday
on the weekend

Monday
Tuesday
Wednesday
Thursday
Friday
Saturday
Sunday

Unit 6

cook
dance
draw
drive
play the guitar
play the piano
ride a bike
sing
speak another language
speak French
speak Korean
speak Spanish
use a computer

(not) at all
very well
well

at a club
at home
at school
in the neighborhood

Unit 7

boots
jeans
pants
shirt
shorts
skirt
sneakers
suit
sunglasses
sweater
T-shirt

black
blue
brown
green
orange
pink
purple
red
white
yellow

drink
drink a soda
eat
eat a hamburger
eat pizza
listen to music
talk on the phone
talk to somebody
wear (jeans)

cool
cute

athletic clothes
business clothes
casual clothes
formal clothes

Unit 8

bag
bed
book
chair
closet
comic book
computer

curtain
desk
drawer
lamp
sofa
table
window

apartment
bathroom
bedroom
kitchen
living room

brand new
broken
comfortable
old

Unit 9

bank
bookstore
cafe
convenience store
department store
drugstore
furniture store
gas station
library
movie theater
park
parking lot
police station
post office
public restrooms
subway station
traffic lights

across from
between
near
next to
on the corner of

cross (Main Street)
go straight on (Main Street)
turn left/right at the corner
turn left/right on (Main
   Street)

Unit 10

apples
bananas
bread
cake
chicken
coffee
cookies
dessert
drinks
fish
food
fruit
ice cream
juice
lettuce
milk
pasta
potatoes
recipe
refrigerator
rice
sandwich
snack
stove
tea

a large pizza
a medium pizza
a slice of pizza
a small pizza

Unit 11

the doctor's office
the gym
home
the laundromat
the library
the mall
school
the supermarket
work

all day
last night
this morning
yesterday

bored
busy
sick
tired

Unit 12

clean my room
do the laundry
do my homework
go out for dinner
go to a party
go to the beach
hang out with friends
have fun
see a movie
stay home
take a trip
visit family

always
never
often
rarely
sometimes

last summer
on Saturday afternoon
this weekend

crowded
interesting
noisy
sad